Elusiv

ELUSIVE LOVE

Alison L Murtough

Elusive Love

Copyright © July 2011 Alison Louise Murtough

All rights reserved.

ISBN: 1463655827
ISBN-13: 978-1463655822

DEDICATION

With thanks, for her constant love acceptance and sacrifice, to my mother and soul sister Barbra Browne, without whom this book would never have materialized.

With love to my amazing children Matthew, Jodi and Joel, who I consider to be among my greatest teachers and friends.

CONTENTS

	Acknowledgments	i
	Introduction	1
PART I – MASTER TALKS		
1	In The Beginning	6
2	Who or What is Master?	19
3	How Shall I Explain Your Work?	24
4	Time to Wake Up	25
5	Fear	27
6	Confusion	31
7	DNA	34
8	Surrender to Love	37
9	Transformation	40
10	Send Love To War	42
11	Time	43
12	The Council of Nine	45
13	You Have Everything You Need	47
14	Master's Plan	48

PART II – DIALOGUE WITH MASTER

15	Where is Master?	54
16	Channeling of Other Beings	56
17	How Do I Stop Worrying?	62
18	The Army	71
19	Plan for Success	76
20	Become the Commander of Your Mind	82
21	Being Mindful	88
22	Meditation	95
23	Earth – Resurrection or Destruction?	107
24	Ritual	113
25	Honoring Ancestors	115
26	Confused About Confusion	122
27	How Do I Experience Self?	132
28	Clear Communication	135
29	How Do I Help My Children Find Their Direction?	138
30	My Hostile Neighbor	142
31	How Do We Help the Youth?	145

32	Perfection v. Beauty	152
33	Gentle Death	156
34	Looking For Love	161
35	Are Our Lives Pre-Determined?	179
36	A Teenager's Concerns	184
37	How Do I Decide?	195
38	Why Do I Have Pain and Tinnitus?	198
39	Projecting Ideas	200
40	Your Body is a Gift	202
41	A Problem With Alignment	206
42	The Giant Within	212
43	About Creating Our Reality	226
44	About Master's Plan	230
	About The Author	231

ACKNOWLEDGMENTS

To my good friends: Marie Davis for her enduring love, wisdom and endless cups of tea; Alex Wood for her help with editing and "Mary" for her tenacious questioning of Master and recognition and value of the wisdom and love within these pages; and to all those whose dialogue with Master made this book possible.

Thanks also to my eldest son Matt Mansfield of MM Photographics Ltd, UK for his expertise in creating the cover design and photo.

INTRODUCTION

Just as much of my life has unfolded seemingly quite by accident, a few years ago in March 2008, I had, what may appear to some, to be a most unusual experience and yet to others, familiar with the process, my telling of these events may complement their own experiences. During a meditation group I was facilitating my body was, with my complete trust and acceptance, used as a vehicle for an intelligent loving consciousness to speak directly, for the purpose of assisting others to awaken to the experience of living from the heart. This consciousness referred to "himself" as Master and explained that "he" was the master of Lao Tzu and Confucius, and had never been incarnate upon earth, but was the consciousness of the collective soul. "He" said Lao Tzu understood everything and Confucius had asked many questions.

By bringing forth absolute clarity to any question posed, whilst at the same time infusing those who listened with a powerful sense of being in the presence of the divine – Master would regularly speak after and sometimes during our meditation, bringing forth words of wisdom. Master instructed me to record everything. I consider some of the information brought forth in this manner, most especially the chapter on DNA, to be of vital importance to us all.

As we live life most of us very quickly become experts at blocking out the familiar noises in our environment - the "background noise", yet it is there, and we have to make a conscious effort to listen in order to hear those familiar noises. In much the same way that we block out noise, a large proportion of humanity has also blocked out of their awareness the ever present sea of intelligent love which exists within and around us, at all times, a conscious loving energy. We may get glimpses or fleeting sensations of bathing in this sea of consciousness, whether during meditation; practising yoga; being in love; holding a new born baby; listening to music or appreciating the beauty of nature, as we get filled with a sense of wonderment and awe, of something greater, of something desired yet elusive. In the past we have generally accepted that these moments are but fleeting and many have lived their entire lives satisfied that they had, even if only for a moment, experienced love in one or other of its many forms. But we are now living in an age where we have relatively easy access to many spiritual masters and are becoming more and more capable of practising methods of how to not only reach those heightened states of awareness but of living life moment to moment in a state of bliss and love.

At first I did not ask any specific questions at all or ask for any communication with Master. In those early days it seemed that when conditions were right "he" was able to communicate through me. There was a definite sensation within me, a kind of knowing that Master was present and wanted to communicate, so I would hurriedly arm myself with pen and paper, and later on a recording device, or switch the computer on to record as he spoke.

Some of the passages have a totally different style from others and on reflection it appears to me that at the times when I receive information directly from Master, with nobody else present, the information is extremely clear and flowing and the grammar has more structure. Whereas, when I have one or more people with me asking questions, the dialogue from Master has a decidedly broken English flavour and does not have the fluidity of passages as previously referred to. My theory is, that at present, when others are with me the group energy field is denser than my own energy field, and hence the communication is more difficult.

It is my choice to refer to the voice as "he" for ease of explanation. My understanding, as it was later explained to me by Master, is that this energy is a part of the consciousness of us all as a collective, not of a separate being.

I have attempted some sort of order by splitting the book into two halves. The passages of text channelled to me either during the night or while in meditation alone at home are in Part 1 - Master Talks, and excerpts of dialogue between Master and individuals who came for life guidance in Part II - Dialogue With Master.

When Master refers to individuals he does not use names, he says "this one" or "other". Where he refers to me I have put "*this one*" in italics and when in dialogue with someone else who is for example asking questions about another person, "this one" or "other" are the terms Master uses to refer to such a person and they will not be in italics.

The first passage, In The Beginning, was channelled one morning at home after the initial "visit" from Master in our meditation group and it is deliberately spaced out with just a few words on each page so that you have the opportunity to understand and feel the meaning of what is conveyed before carrying on to the next page. Thereafter the dialogues are not in chronological order

I have inserted a short history of my background at the end of the book so that those of you who wish to can get started without having to wade through a lengthy introduction.

PART I

MASTER TALKS

1 IN THE BEGINNING

"In the beginning there was

no sound,

no thought,

no form.

There was only the void.

Everything came out of the void.

Everything that is in our

known and unknown universe

came out of the void.

Within the void there is

a peace,

a stillness

beyond anything known to man,

total serenity.

The void surrenders everything

for

nothing.

The very act of surrendering

created movement.

Movement created sound.

And the combination of

movement and sound

created form.

Thus the world and the universe

came into being.

The quality of the surrendering of the void is love. Each time one breathes out pure love there is a replication of those moments of creation. Each time you surrender to the universe there is movement in your life. It has always been so and will always be so.

We are at a stage in the evolution of mankind where chaos reigns supreme on earth. Even the "leaders" need to be led. They are in a state of panic and do everything on a wing and a prayer. The only way out of the current dilemma presently facing society is to listen to the voices of the soul.

The voices of the soul come to you on earth in many guises. They speak only the truth and their only purpose is to assist mankind in returning to an existence nothing short of heavenly bliss. A world where neighbor helps neighbor and love is felt to pervade everything.

When a whisper has the power of truth behind it –

IT BECOMES A ROAR!

Not one person on earth will be able to ignore the power of this spoken word. And the power is love and the words are truth.

The voices of the soul arise when reason has been lost. They offer help when the path of love has been forgotten. They affect every heart that hears them. They are salvation. They are the solution to the present unrest.

The voices of the soul belong to you. They are the part of you that did not forget love. They do not come from an outside source. They are not angelic beings. They are eternal wisdom and show you the way back to your heart.

An uncluttered mind, an open heart and a servant of the divine is the doorway that is needed for the voices of the soul to be able to be heard.

One such has come to the world to light the way for others – to be courageous enough to show the world that this is the answer they are seeking and then many more will appear that have, until now, been hiding. Many more, who have been quietly working, will now be heard the world over. Yes my dear, that one such is you. We will explain in detail the process so that others will understand and more readily accept this new way of learning and re-learning of loving and re-loving of living life not merely existing, of enjoying themselves and others.

LOVE IS ALL YOU NEED!

Only in solitude can you

realize your magnitude.

Only in solitude can you meet the divine presence who is yourself, who walks with you every step of the way - the part of you that came from the void, the part of you that is love.

In quiet contemplation of all that is divine - neither yours nor mine - the whole that is perfection, seen only upon reflection.

So my dear, we have spoken about creation – movement, then sound, then form. Now the next question is "From where did consciousness arise?"

Consciousness arose from two great minds.

Mind is movement. The void had movement and creation had movement.

The combining of the movement from the void and the movement from the creation, which emanated from the void, created consciousness.

Mind is the product of the conflict of the consciousness of the void and the consciousness of creation.

That is why there is so much conflict in the mind.

The proportion of the unconscious mind to the conscious mind is directly related to the void and the creation in form.

The motion of the unconscious mind is exactly the same as the void and constantly expresses its desire for emptiness by depositing any excess in the conscious mind.

But the conscious mind needs to allow the flow to continue uninterrupted and needs to express itself in sound and form.

If mind does not find an outlet to express itself then there is created a "dam" and much pressure is present in the mind.

This pressure causes all of mankind's problems. It causes all mental conditions from the very mild to the very extreme.

So the mind observes the mechanics of creation and the heart feels the quality of the void, which is giving everything for nothing and is love.

When mind understands its essence, it can never be deceived again.

The only way mind can be controlled is to believe that falsehoods are real.

So, to understand that the reality of the power of uninterrupted flow from the void is exactly the same flow that powers mankind is to understand everything.

The two opposing movements which create mind, form duality. Everything in nature is born from two; everything that is birthed is birthed from two. Everything that exists, exists not only in duality but from duality. The brain itself is in two and has opposite attributes and functions. Duality was birthed from one, from the void, when the void expressed the quality of love with its giving of everything to remain nothing.

Consciousness expresses itself in sound and form.

When Master speaks the sound expresses the consciousness of Master.

When Alison speaks her sound expresses her consciousness.

Consciousness of Master is not the same as consciousness of Alison.

It must be clear to those who listen when Master speaks. If the voices sound the same it would not be clear if words come from Master or from Alison's mind.

Wisdom of Master is accessible to everyone.

Wisdom of Alison is only accessible to Alison.

This is true leadership.

When people listen to Master they need nothing more for they get everything.

2 WHO OR WHAT IS MASTER?

One day my daughter had asked me the question "What is the difference between a schizophrenic and what you do?" It made me wonder and I had no immediate reply for her. When I found some time later in the day to meditate whilst the house was quiet I asked Master and the reply was:

M: When a schizophrenic speaks only the schizophrenic understands – when Master speaks everyone understands.

There was a pause in the channeling and I had this question in mind:

Alison: *Are you part of myself?*

M: Yes my dear, Master is part of you, but also part of everyone.

Everyone who has a connection with Master can talk directly without you.

So Master is not a bit of you that you have not admitted to.

Master is the part of you that is also a part of everyone – the Voice of the Soul. You understand?

People try to give form to consciousness of the soul. It is difficult for them to accept spoken words. People's experience is of form and to understand things, they look more closely at form, using a microscope even to look deeper.

So when they hear the message from Master they look for form, from habit, they think that if there is a form that they can understand more the message.

But there is no form; there has never been a form. Try to think of the sky. Clouds give the sky form but without clouds what is sky. So Master is consciousness without form.

People think when they hear the words of Master that it must be a person speaking because that is their experience, they have only ever heard beings like themselves using sound in this way. This is a new experience for many people, but also there are many people who do this already and they will now have the courage to say "I do that also, here I am", and these people will help us when they have the courage to speak their truth to the world.

No, the voices come as an expression of the Consciousness of the Soul of your world and more than your world.

It is time to speak directly as time is short and things must now move quickly, for everyone to change quickly, for everyone to realize themselves, and who and what they are.

Never talk Master magic. Master is not magic. Master is for everyone, everyone my dear. If you talk magic then many people think that Master is not for them. Master is for everyone, Master is like the wind and the sun, the sky and the trees, the earth and the oceans. All these things are for everyone and everyone accept these things, so please never talk of Master like magic.

Master is the voice of common reason, the voice of understanding, the keeper of the knowledge of all things.

Master is not a man or a woman, not an angel or a guide – no, not in any form known to man.

Man only understands if things appear in form, in pattern. Even if Master appeared only as sound, man would be frightened, so man does not even understand sound, only form.

So people try to believe that Master (is) Alison. No my dear, Master is not only Alison. Little bit Alison, little bit everyone. Everyone can talk Master and Alison job to teach how to talk Master self. When people learn how to talk Master, Alison job finished.

Some people will ask so is Master God? And Master say "No". Everyone believes that the universe was created by "God". So, Master is consciousness and was born from the mind of the void and the mind of creation. Master is global consciousness, the Master mind as a whole, the engine of the thoughts of mankind and because the energy which feeds Master is love from the void. Master helps everybody.

When people pray, Master hears prayers and Master helps, even if people pray to others it is always Master that hears the prayers and helps. Master does not answer every question as you might expect. No my dear, Master answers question in way to lead you back to your heart. This is purpose of Master - only purpose of Master.

Do not be tempted to call Master by other names as this will confuse. When all people talk with Master then all people understand and are clear. Do not attach any importance to meaning of word, it is simply the expert of the consciousness of global unity and does not imply in any way at all that subservience or obeyance are required. Never follow the one who Master uses to teach you. As soon as you have your connection with Master, please talk directly to Master and let go of the friend who helped you find Master. Understand?

When Alison is quiet it is easy for us to come in and speak because there is no obstruction. Sound causes an obstruction for Master to speak. Master does not like sound like thunder when speaking. When Alison talk, Master goes.

Alison listen every word Master speak, it is OK - little bit inquisitive, little bit control. She like to be careful Master does not say bad thing. But Master only love people, every word spoken with love, only love.

Some people talk God. If we talk God we confuse many people. So some people experience God and they know, and Master does not have to explain. Others just experience self and then they will understand and then there will be no questions about God because everyone will experience and understand everything. So we do not talk God and no confuse.

Fran: *We were wondering, if you have not been present on earth in a physical body what makes you choose to use the Chinese accent that you use?*

M: Very simple. Master talk many time people like this, understand? Many time people like this, one reason. Another reason, when Master talk *you know* Master talk, very simple. Very simple. My dears, everything very simple. Master talk people same talk like this, and when Master talk same they understand but if Master talk like *this one* people no listen.

Fran: *So if you were to come through someone in China would you choose a completely different accent again?*

M: No my dear. No reason. In China people understand! They do not question. They have wisdom, many 1000 years' wisdom, they understand already.

Fran: *OK.*

Fran: *Oh, it's completely perfect. Just every single answer is spot on. The bit about the Chinese voice is so simple so perfect. If he spoke like you no one would listen. Oh, that was just great. That was just great!*

3　HOW SHALL I EXPLAIN YOUR WORK?

After a lengthy channeling session during the day, where one client constantly asked questions like "I need to give notice on my flat by 3 weeks' time if I get this job. Will I get this job by ......such and such date? Or, what country will I live in? All the questions were about how her life would turn out, as if she had no influence on her future, even though Master explained why there had been no progress in her life and what had to be done to correct this problem and hasten positive change – she still continued to ask questions as if Master were a fortune teller. I asked Master the following question later that evening:

Alison: *How shall I explain how you work?*

And the immediate answer was:

M: Master cleans canvas. Master does not paint picture.

4 TIME TO WAKE UP

M: For many years you know that you only use a very small part of your brain. When you have connection with Master you will learn how to use all of your brain. This has not been possible before because the brain is such a powerful tool for you that without love and wisdom there would be chaos, more chaos than there is now. So when everybody has the connection with Master they will learn new ways to use their brain and the parts of the brain they have never used before. This is how things will change very quickly, because people will begin to use their brains to help each other on grand scale, like has never been seen before.

My dear it is as though your world has been sleeping and lately having a nightmare, and now it is time to wake up. You see how different sleeping and nightmares are from your life during the daytime? This is exactly how different world will be for you when everyone wakes up their heart!

The first step is to quiet the mind and answer the questions in the mind until there are no more questions. People come to Master with many, many questions and Master see only one problem. Like a table laid out with many things, you see many problems and then Master looks under table and it looks like a triangle standing on its point, and the point is where the problem is. So Master explain this one problem and all other problems are fixed. Simple. When all questions are answered it is possible for mind to be quiet and then you will feel heart. Sometimes little adjustments are needed for the energy in the body to flow easily and to talk to the fear in the body until it is not afraid anymore.

5 *FEAR*

M: Fear only exists in the mind. Fear is when a part of you falls back into the void. The movement of the void enables creation, so as soon as you fall back into the void mind begins to create reasons for fear, it creates explanations in form, it sees pictures in the mind to explain the fear. Then fear persists because mind tricks it into believing that the pictures in the mind are real and the real cause of the fear, so there is more fear.

Fear arises when the mind loses control of its reality. Mind knows about the void and knows that if mind falls into the void, then mind disappears. The mind has no concept of the experience of the void which is totally opposite to the experience of the mind. The mind only experiences moment by moment and the moment it enters the void it panics, not realizing that the void's only purpose is to keep emptying. So as soon as self experiences just one moment of the void there is fear and panic because the mind is afraid of annihilation. But the void does not want the mind and immediately sends mind away. So in truth mind need not be afraid of the void because the void only wants to remain empty.

Sometimes people do not want to do something so in a moment of hesitation they fall into the void and experience fear. Then they associate the most recent thought as being the cause of the fear. They attach the experience of fear to the thought and it looks like a ball of black the size of a house in front of them and they hide behind it. They do not want to take action they do not want to take responsibility for own life.

Fear arises and the mind projects the fear and creates something which it can relate to in life. Mind does not understand fear and must have an explanation – a focus for the fear. So because mind projected the situation from fear when you send love to the situation/person they act as a mirror and reflect the love back to the very source of the fear within – and this dissolves the fear! .

Life is very simple, there is no mystery but children are never made aware of the simple recipe for a happy life. They are thrown to the lions and their parents say – "Oh, it will make a man of him" – or "It is character building". Is this the act of a loving parent? A loving parent teaches their children, cares for their children and enables their children to create a more loving society, a more just and equitable society.

So my dears the first thing to impart to your children is that they will always be looked after and loved so they do not have to fear, they do not have to worry. You tell them that they are like the flowers and the trees. They need food (earth) and water and love (sun) and they will grow into magnificent beings. You show them the buds on the flowers and see if they can guess what the bud will become. They do not know, they have not ever seen this flower before, and you say to them yes my child you are like this flower – you will grow and one day you will surprise and delight everybody because you will become radiant in showing to the world your full potential. Remember that every seed already has its own template of becoming and being. You never have to try to be like somebody else – just continue to feed yourself and give and receive love and you cannot help but blossom into a radiant human being. When you live life like a flower or a tree you always fulfill your purpose, and at the end of your life you will be very content because you were not squashed and you were not prevented from growing and being who you came to this earth to be.

But you say to Master "But Master what should I do, I must do something? I must train to be a doctor or a lawyer or a bus driver. Only train to do these things if when you think of them your heart explodes with joy, and then when you find what makes your heart sing then you will do that job like an expert because you love to do it.

Children need to feel safe in the world. Do not feed them with your fears. You would not feed them with poison so do not feed them with fear. Fear prevents joy and love. Fear destroys the quality of life. For those that seek to control you then fear is the best weapon they have because you then behave like an obedient slave who fears reprisal at every movement. If you wish to live to your fullest potential replace fear with love. Fear happens when you breathe in and do not breathe out and you fear death. But remember the void, the void has to remain empty and when you fall into the void it sends you back out. It is the same with the breath, when you breathe in then you must breathe out. So if you forget and do not breathe out and feel the darkness of the void and perceive it as fear then just breathe out and concentrate on regulating your breathing – breathe in and out, rhythmically and you will feel a sense of calm and fear will go. So teach your children how to respond when they feel fear.

6 CONFUSION

At meditation circle one evening Master began speaking right at the beginning. He was eager to speak and my foot began furiously tapping on the floor as soon as we all sat down, which is often the way my body reacts as channeling begins. During this channeling when Master says "this one" he is always referring to me. During the week I had been struggling with the thought of returning to work in the commercial world as my income was almost non-existent at times. I would often reproach myself for not having studied for a degree thereby setting myself up with a regular income and the security of a pension. Even though I could never bring myself to follow this kind of 'normal' life I would often think I had made wrong decisions; that I was doing what I wanted to do and maybe it wasn't what I ought to be doing from a socially acceptable and sensible view point. I have since gladly accepted that my service to the world is to bring forth Master's wisdom.

M: Much confusion. Much confusion in world. Even *this one* confused. Even *this one* very confused, because confusion in air. You breathe confusion, everyone breathe confusion. Very destructive, like weapon. First people confuse, then people lose control, they do not understand why confused, they do not understand. Everybody feel, they cannot see reason why things change. So they run like frightened little rabbits. They do not know where they run. They run because they are frightened, confused. When you feel confused you must remember you feel confusion from world. So you must separate yourself from this confusion and you must realize what is happening so you do not become like frightened rabbit.

People think when they have problem only is their problem - but no my dear everything happen in world now become everybody problem because everyone feel same. They feel things from many different places they feel things from many different people.

So they become confused and they do not realize they are like antennae - they feel everything from everybody and then they look for someone to blame so they blame whoever they can and they start to fight, they start to argue. They become very discontent, more confusion. When they blame someone else, little bit more clarity for them for they think they find reason for confusion - but no, illusion, this is why people always have to blame someone else because they think they find little clarity but this is not solution. Must become like conductor, first you become aerial - you receive signal everybody so you feel everything (from) everybody so you must become conductor, you must let this pass through you. You feel confused - realize does not belong to you, so you let pass through like wind in trees, OK? Tree very strong, tree bend in wind, tree disperse wind. Understand. Tree disperse wind, so you must let confusion pass through you and through this understanding you disperse confusion. *This one* should know better, but no, even *this one* confuse. She think own problem! No! This problem world. This problem world. You must become like tree and disperse wind, disperse confusion. Tree teach you everything. Tree very clever, tree teach you everything. This is why tree so big, this is why tree so big, so you notice tree. You notice tree, but nobody notice tree. So this is problem, this is problem in world. So we must teach people how to be like tree, how to disperse wind, disperse confusion. Very difficult for Master when *this one* confuse, not impossible, but difficult.

7 DNA

M: Master wants to talk about biosynthesis. For many years biodiversity is unchanged. Sometimes it is allowed for changes to happen. But in recent years people have manipulated the DNA of plants, of marine life and even of animals. Manipulating DNA has consequences which change the entire cosmos. Like the plates of the earth can move and then there is an earthquake, so when the DNA is changed, this is changing the fabric of the universe. DNA is a representation of the whole of creation. So when DNA is changed there is created a fault line like when there is an earthquake on earth, and you know the consequences of earthquake! The whole of creation happened because there was perfect order – PERFECT ORDER. So if the expression of that perfect order is tampered with at the fundamental level of DNA man creates disorder. This is one of the major reasons why there is such disorder in the world today. People feel that there have been deliberate changes in the DNA of the food they eat and so they are fighting for survival. My dears they do not understand when they fight for survival the reason, so they fight each other. The problem of a few becomes the problem of everybody, because there is only one consciousness, there is only one mind. There have been terrible inhuman experiments done on humans and the results have always been catastrophic for their minds. How much more catastrophic then my dears do you think that to tamper with the very foundation of creation, the blue print of humanity, the order of the universe even – and then people look at the chaos and disorder in the world and wonder what is occurring.

Correction can take place if before you eat your food you place it on top of the original design for 10 minutes. This is long enough for your food to adjust and to remember. The design is not the spiral of DNA that you are accustomed to associating with DNA but it is the very core design of the hexagon – the repeating hexagon – like honeycomb. This is for small quantities like when each individual partakes of nutrition at various times in the day. This is the best way to re-balance the food that you eat; also, you will find that people remain healthy. People who do not engage in open conflict with each other will show symptoms of conflict within themselves because of the disorder within the DNA in the world, so to eat food which has sat upon a honeycomb design will restore order in the body and mind. Yes my dears even in the mind. Many people think they are going crazy. They think irrational thoughts, they are suicidal. There is much suicide and it is increasing. This is a consequence of the disorder, so the honeycomb design will even help these people and create order and peace in their minds.

Note: This is the hexagon pattern to use. You can access this design from my website www.voicesofthesoul.com. I suggest laminating it to use on your kitchen worktop or in your refrigerator or ideally both.

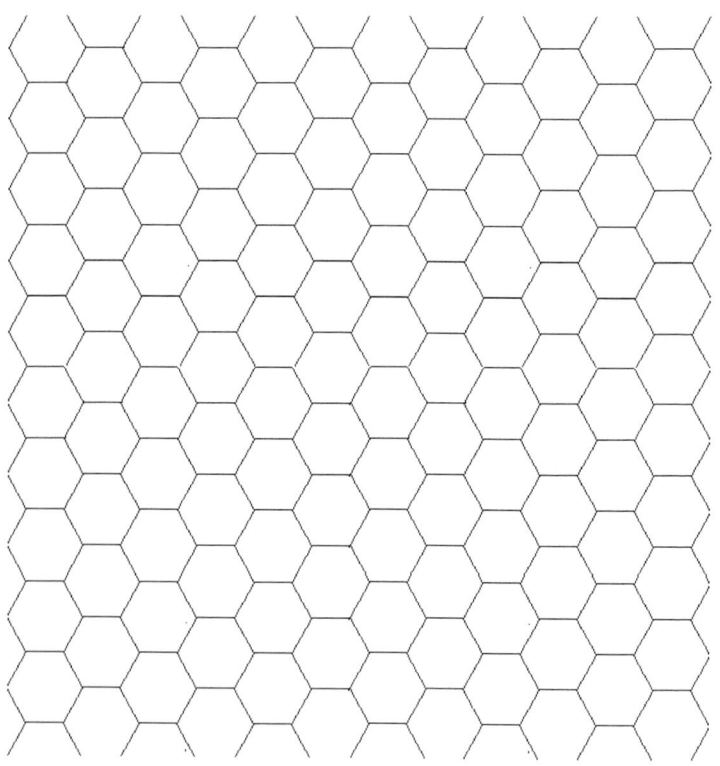

8 SURRENDER TO LOVE

In meditation with our regular group I observed that we were all given a solar disk energetic transmission into our bodies which was a disk imprinted or embossed with codes and was told that we would be receiving a lot of information for translation for ourselves and also we would transmit information for others. Master referred to the transmission of the disk as a device.

M: My dear we are eager to work with you to bring many benefit to all of mankind. Our little device will enable clear communication of many things that previously were very difficult to explain because you will have total complete understanding and then the ability to translate this knowledge into language that you are able to understand and that others will understand also. Codes are direct experience, device is receptacle for codes. So now you have ability to transmit much information to many people.

You have been very concerned about transmitting information from Master to many people and you feel that your availability for others is under-utilized. Master has told you before, preparation. Master prepare everybody. You worry finance for self. Master say to you do not worry but you worry, worry, worry. You think Master does not understand finance. But no, Master understand finance is of importance to you. Finance not important for Master but Master realize importance for self. But, if you could have experience same Master you would not worry finance, if you understand then you no more worry finance because this worry finance create like fishing net around you and keep you trapped; trapped with other people; trapped with self; trapped with mind. Very small experience of world when trapped in fishing net. When liberated, then experience limitless. Limitless my dear, and because limitless, you get everything you require. Because you never experience this limitless before, you cannot comprehend to live without worry finance. So to achieve this experience you must surrender your life to Master work. When you surrender life to Master work, Master always look after you, Master always direct you to best possible outcome for self. Direct you to happy heart direct you to love self. Many people lost in pain, in tears, in anguish. Even they see no way out of their situation. You have come to world to reassure these people that there is a way out of their misery and to show them the way out of their misery. We show them the way out of their misery.

When they say they have no one to love them we show them Master's love. They feel Master's love and they become full of love for self. They become like sun in sky and shine love to everybody. Then they forget anguish, they forget fear and they forget loneliness; they only feel love in heart and they forget mind.

Mind become voluntary prisoner of heart. Mind feels heart look after mind, so mind very comfortable, does not have to worry. Mind can relax and lay on soft clouds in heart."

9 TRANSFORMATION

M: Everything is ready for expansion. Everyone is poised on the brink of incredible transformation. Transformation in mind and transformation in body. This is why people are so agitated, they feel there is great change in air, they anticipate that life will never be the same again. And they are correct, but they are used to catastrophe so they envisage catastrophe. No my dear no catastrophe, only incredible transformation. The best way to make this transition is to be very clear that outcome will be positive for everyone and to relax and breathe in rhythm with each other. When you all breathe in rhythm together then transformation happen with least resistance. So begin with family and practice to breathe in rhythm each other, then when you find this very simple to do practice with other people. Just like when you stop mind and Master can talk, so, when you stop breath Master can sing. Master does not mean (*you*) to stop breathing, but in-between breath out and breath in there is a moment when Master can sing - very easy for Master - and when everybody create same moment this is moment for great transformation.

Master is very aware that there is much confusion in world this is why Master talk to you, this is why Master explain everything to you to make clear process to assist transformation.

You see, when you cannot communicate other people with mind and with information, then when you practice breathing together, when these people are nearby they automatically begin to breathe in synchronization with you. So Master can sing to everybody and everybody feel love from Master and from self and from each other – everybody feel love all time. This is transformation.

10 *SEND LOVE TO WAR*

M: Now we talk war, war is confusion, many minds confused. They forget love, yes my dear, they forget self. When Master see war, Master contain war. Is better than war all over world. People do crazy things and Master has to think of everyone. If people not fighting, send love to people fighting then war stop. Many people look at war and do not like what they see so they send negative thoughts to people in war, no my dear they must send love to people in war and war will stop. They are lost, they need love. Now in this world there are many wars, one war stops and five more wars start, then people worry, worry, worry. They worry earth; they worry food, no my dear they make war worse. They must send love, not worry. When people wake up very quickly they send love to war and war stop.

11 *TIME*

M: There is a common misconception that time does not exist. Time does exist because you created it. You create your reality and you have created time. You could change the shape of the cosmos but you have not even considered to do this. "When time began" signifies an assumption that there was a period before time when there was no time and this is correct. Before time there was timelessness. No one moment could be distinguished from any other moment. The consciousness present at timelessness was not aware of any passing of time hence there was timelessness.

Then as man evolved and began to live his life as separate beings and began to interact with others and organize his world and his life he also found that organizing time was of benefit to his activities. He could assume more order if the element of time was involved, and there was a great need to order, because order had been lost. When there is total order there is timelessness, there is serenity; there is understanding; but it is not felt as being separate because there is only the consciousness being consciousness in no time. The shift from order to disorder is a natural cyclic occurrence and conveys no "deep" meaning save that it maintains the balance necessary for the continuation of the cosmos and beyond the cosmos. There is no benefit in trying to understand what causes the shift although there are those of you who insist on knowing everything and we would explain to you that there are layers within the universe which when in close proximity to other layers resonate in harmony with them and there are layers which do not resonate in harmony so when one layer is not resonating in harmony over a prolonged period there is collapse and disorder is the result. Consciousness is separate from the layers. Consciousness perceives the layers much like you perceive the wind - not the wind - the air currents. Consciousness can expand into the layers and experience them as separate or integrate them into itself and unite in one. In fact, it is usual that consciousness feels the difference in the layers as it moves to integrate them.

12   THE COUNCIL OF NINE

In several previous meditations over the years I had come across reference to The Council of Nine and not knowing anything about them asked Master to explain who or what they were.

M: The Council of Nine are a group of beings with one representative from each of the nine dimensions that support separate identity consciousness. Beyond the 9th dimension there is no separateness, there is unity of thought and feeling. There is no distinction between one thought and another thought. The nine dimensions are also what you on earth refer to as the 9th harmonic convergence. The Council of Nine orchestrate harmony between these dimensions. They are constantly on guard for any collapse and immediately set forth to rectify disharmonious proportions to the whole of creation. The Council of Nine are the guardians, the gatekeepers of consciousness reality. They have been enlisted to ensure order in number is maintained. Where number is corrupted collapse is inevitable. So harmony rests solely on perfect geometric stability in each dimension and within relationship of each dimension to all other dimensions. The universe is finely tuned and will continue to breathe as long as this order is maintained.

There has been misuse of power at times which has caused near apocalyptic catastrophe and damage to the grids which stabilize the very foundation of the cosmos. It is these grids which are currently under reconstruction and resurrection. Some grids have remained hidden for safety as there were those that were only intent on their destruction. But now it is time to repair and rebuild. This truly is a momentous time in the history of your universe.

The Council of Nine are great mathematicians. They are revered as are elders in your society. Master is not concerned with these beings as they are responsible for the grids and for harmony and they specialize entirely for this purpose and their only reason for existence is to complete their mission with no distraction. They entirely live their purpose and their purpose is to ensure continuity of mankind, of universe and of order of universe.

13 *YOU HAVE EVERYTHING YOU NEED*

M: Master is like the conductor and you, all the people are like the orchestra, but most of the orchestra have their instruments sitting idle in their lap. When each and every one of you play the song of love with your instrument (your heart) and follow the direction of Master, then all will be in harmony and the sound will be divine. You see my children you already have everything you need.

You all want to know what your jobs will be. What would you like to do? Huh? You didn't expect us to say that did you. Well what do you want to do? What do you enjoy doing? You see there is no rush, there is rush and there is no rush. If you look at a flower before it is a flower and you wait, you wait for long time and then there is a flower. But if you're busy and not looking at the flower then the flower comes all of a sudden and you didn't expect it. That is what is happening in your world. All of a sudden everyone will be smiling and you didn't expect it to happen, but it will happen, so – do what you enjoy to do. You are like our children, do what you enjoy to do and then one day everyone's hearts will be open like the flowers. People have forgotten to be like the children, they have forgotten so many things.

14 MASTER'S PLAN

Mary and I had been drinking tea and talking about what questions to ask Master. What was the plan to take the work forward and how we could let as many people as possible know etc. The channeling session began with much tapping of my feet, so much so that it sounded like a seal flapping its tail! Master had previously explained a useful method of using our brain by communicating to it as though it were your own personal army and he refers here again to the army but this time it is his army.

M: Master very excited, very exhilarate, Master already begin army. Army wait instructions. Not everybody prepared yet, not everybody ready now, army is in process of attaining a structure, this takes little time for new recruit. You see, if you want to defend castle you need one each corner, otherwise defense not strong, same structure for army Master, for purpose change world, OK? So Master have exactly precise quantity, precise quantity individual, because each individual have particular purpose and each individual have different purpose, when they synchronize at precisely the required interval then change happen in less than second. This is Master plan. So army begin formulate, structure become visible little, little, need more individual. Prepare individual purpose, individual purpose not everybody same. Then when everybody prepare, then they will know they have job to do, but, at moment preparation, at moment preparation each individual. Do not worry purpose, do not worry direction, everything happen in perfect order, perfect order. If too quickly people get frightened - run away, cannot have army of frightened rabbit. Yes? So we go little slowly, little slowly not too slowly so preparation complete, no chance for error. At precise time everyone prepared everyone in specific location even, then in less than second entire world change. Entire world change.

Mary: *Magic!*

M: Yes my dear, because people do not expect, because they do not know exact individual purpose until exactly precise moment arrive. So even for them magic, even for them magic. If they know beforehand, mind confuse, mind create obstruction and process become slow, very slow, even so slow does not happen, OK? Many people in own way organize, organize, *this one* need more word, *this one* need more word.

Eventually, Master explain, eventually, but you understand slice, slice, slice, each slice is structure. Each slice structure, each structure has people who organize. When every slice in place, even every slice become joined together, each slice become joined together, then become incredible structure. Even people create slice they have not capability create complete phenomenal structure, so they create slice, then when time join together, this is how in less than second world change. At moment each slice very separate, each slice listen own idea, they think they know what they do, and they do know what they do, but they only know slice, so Master know exactly order slice for maximum effect. For maximum effect, phenomenal change, so in less than one second people integrate, integrate slice, not even this way because slice not mixed together, slice not mixed together. Slice connect together. People understand geometry. Geometry very important for this one. Structure slice by slice. So you do not worry purpose. Do not worry nothing even, because all you need to do for world is enjoy life, become very clear. Do not go into dark room; do not worry (*about*) other people. Love self only, love self. Then you become like sun in sky, very big, very bright, very bright. Sun never stop shining…..never stop shining.

OK, now you understand Master plan, now you understand Master preparation happen. You understand, you do not worry individual purpose because only when time is precise moment you will understand purpose and in same moment change. Instantaneous phenomena. Because you do not have time for mind to change. Instant understanding, same moment everybody, mind not quick enough, so phenomena happen. Instantaneous phenomena. Instantaneous phenomena. Unbelievable instantaneous phenomena. Even words sound like music when you talk this thing because music everything, world change. Will hear music, everything in order, you do not listen confusion no more, only music, only music.

Master sings

"Bea-u-ti-ful in-stan-tan-eous phe-nom-en-a!"

Elusive Love

PART II

DIALOGUE WITH MASTER

15   WHERE IS MASTER?

Linda: *Hello Master.*

M: Master very happy to see you today. Very happy, very happy. Welcome welcome welcome.

Linda: *I always feel better when I am in your presence and I suppose I am struggling feeling I am not in your presence all the time.*

M: This is illusion, this is illusion. Where is Master?

Linda: *Everywhere. Intellectually that makes sense to me. I don't know why I am putting resistance up.*

M: My dear Master is self also. You have body, you have eye, you have finger, you have toe, you have arm, you have leg – you have Master! Same Same Same. So you can, if for you more easy to understand, more easy to remember Master, you can imagine Master live in pocket. Ha!

Linda: *OK.*

M: Master does not go away!

Linda: *I think I have been in a big habit of being in a space of negativity.*

M: Yes my dear this is habit. You believe life miserable. So if you want life happy remember Master pocket. Ha Ha Ha. Master pocket! Do not forget. This create problem for this one because she think to self "I have so many clothes, sometimes no pocket". My dear when you wear clothes (*with*) pocket you will observe more happy. Ha Ha OK?

Linda: *Yes thank you.*

16 CHANNELLING OF OTHER BEINGS

Mary is one of my good friends. She was with me when I visited Mother Meera the week before the channeling began. She seemed to have endless questions for Master and we met up not only for our meditation meetings but also during the week specifically to ask Master questions.

Mary has studied many religions and read extensively on spiritual matters. Probably because she had read so much on different religions and been involved with various organizations Mary desperately needed not only clarity but a true experience that would give her certainty of the presence of the divine. Her personal experiences have been profound at times and disturbing at other times and she instantly recognized the value of what was being made available to us all through this connection with the divine. Our first session of enquiry began thus:

Mary: *We have been wondering for some time now, because there is so much channeling going on in the world today. People say they are channeling different information from different Archangels and what they call ascended Masters. Now a lot of information is coming into the world and sometimes it is conflicting. We would like to know if it is* *confused information or is it the people that are interpreting it that are confusing the information that is coming through?*

M: This question very imprecise. Not very direct. Many people talk, say different thing, you in the world have many different languages, yes? People use different word, some people do not understand. Same when people talk. Same when people talk. You think, conflicting information OK? But, information not important. Information not important. Surprise you! Information not important because people who listen particular information, OK, information like key in door. Only important is that door open. Not important information. So yes, conflicting information, different language, people understand different things. So they get confused. They think "Oh, this information different from this information so this information invalid", but no my dear, because key in door only – does not matter information one little bit. Understand?

Mary: *Sorry Master, how I understood it was that all the information coming through from these higher beings is correct, that they have a higher purpose.*

M: All information purpose to open door for people. Information like key. People need key for door. Different key open different door so information not important. Only important door open. So depend people understanding, depend people philosophy, depend people religion, depend many things, many things depend upon information they listen to OK?

Mary: *Right.*

M: If someone have idea something, very strong idea, they only listen something make that idea feel very comfortable for them. OK, does not matter. No importance, does not matter content of information. Only matter outcome - door open for them. Many people like to eat different things, outcome they have full stomach, so not important what they eat, same information. Not important at all. Too much importance attached to importance of information. Has no importance at all. You see when everybody understand inside, when everybody understand with no word, no need for any information, information obsolete – so information no importance, no importance at all. Ha!

Mary: *Thank you Master. My personal consideration is that I have been in so many different religious disciplines, I have read so much, I have been to all sorts of people to get information, the light from Master whatever, and it just didn't bring me to connect ….*

M: Yes problem you, you too many path. This is only problem. If you walk down road, you have one foot one side, one foot other side - you get knocked down by car! So this is problem for you. Too many conflicting information confuse mind because you do not realize, you stay on one path only it does not matter which path, does not matter which path. You change path because you feel uncomfortable, or you change path because you very curious or because you find information very confusing but you confuse more, you confuse more, you think always grass greener. You have expression grass greener. This is your problem. You think something else better, then you try to catch this thing and get confused. Nothing invalid, nothing invalid. Even when some people perceive some religion, some philosophy they perceive to be totally crazy, they do not understand one little bit, not important because people who involve this philosophy understand everything.

Note: On a separate occasion whilst at home I asked Master for an explanation about people who channel other "beings".

I have never held beliefs about angels, other dimensions or any of the many other weird and wonderful experiences people have had and which seem to go hand in hand with today's concept of spirituality. Even during my healing practice I maintain a certain detachment from forming beliefs around what I observe energetically. As our brains are capable of inventing realities, stories and dreams it always seemed to me that, as the expression goes, a picture paints a 1000 words, whatever I saw or others saw could just be constructed from the mind in order to provide an explanation of the way things were and prevent fears arising due to not knowing. It seemed that people could not cope without boundaries, and belief systems provided boundaries for the mind just like a cup provides a boundary, a container, for the liquid it carries. However, I thought it may be that there are in reality other beings from other dimensions seeing as now I am involved in dialogue with something which appears to be a separate consciousness, even though it has explained that it is not separate. It's like two sides of the same coin.

M: These people have certain abilities and are in need of representation of self to explain knowledge, new knowledge. Because they require representation of self they specialize. Master motivates this experience for them. But for you my dear you do not need representation of self, so you understand Master and you do not specialize, you do not have fixed ideas, never. So Master is able to communicate you everything for everybody and everybody understand everything. People who specialize work for individual and Master choose these people to work for individual, but Master has job to do for world so Master use you to help world, not so much individual but world. This is why not so many individuals know you. You will remain anonymous to many people. They will read Master's book and they will begin to understand many things. And when they begin to understand many things they become less serious, they realize life is very simple, they remember priorities.

Because responsibility has been taken away from individuals they are in confusion. They have no priorities because they have no responsibilities. They do not have to hunt for their food, they do not have to grow their food, they do not have to look after parents even, if they choose they do not have to look after their children. If they choose even they do not have to go to work. So if there are not definite responsibilities how can there be definite priorities? When people have definite responsibilities then they become aware of consequences. When they have an awareness of consequences they begin to have awareness of their actions.

17 HOW DO I STOP WORRYING?

Helen: *How do I stop worrying?*

M: When you realize consequence of worry you very quickly stop worrying.

Helen: *I am always worrying and I know there is no point in worrying.*

M: No my dear, to say there is no point to worry is not enough reason to stop worry. This is why you do not stop worry. If you realize exactly consequence of worry you never worry again. Worry prevent progress, prevent success, prevent love even, is like, people say cloud, no not like cloud, look like cloud, but the effect of worry is to have self imprisoned in room with wall concrete even 100 feet thick. This is what worry does, it keeps you imprisoned from life itself. When you stop to worry life change completely. Everything you concern, everything you worry, things you do not want disappear, things you want come to you. Very simple. Very simple. When you do not worry you get everything.

Helen: *So if you worry about money it will stop coming to you?*

M: Yes my dear. Worry nothing. Worry nothing get everything. Very simple. Remember 100 feet concrete if you worry,

Helen: *OK.*

M: People do not realize what they do.

Helen: *How can I help other people not to worry then?*

M: My dear do not worry other people. Because when you do not worry then life give you everything to make you happy, you become like sun. Sun does not say look at me I am sun, everybody see sun, everybody feel sun, no need to worry other people because they see you and they understand just by your life.

Helen: *OK. Thank you.*

Mary: *What about me having this constant worry when I look at the world today? Like last night when I look at the TV program like Al Jazeera which tells us exactly what is going on and it really looks like a total mess and I know you said you have everything under control and that ……..*

M: You think Master not capable?

Mary: *Master is capable; I am not questioning that …*

M: Do not worry, Master very capable. It is precisely because mess, Master come. Precisely this reason. If people happy no need Master teach. OK?

Mary: *Yes I understand.*

M: You worry my dear, this world at moment appear beyond redemption.

Mary: *Yes.*

M: But you look through own eye. When Master look at problem Master has Master perspective. OK. When you have Master eye you understand process, you understand severity of situation completely and you have capability precise action. Precise moment to effect change.

Mary: *Right.*

M: Everybody has own purpose and you spend much time and energy to look at problem in world, does not serve you. This stop own happy. This stop experience love. You must become like fountain and instead of water in fountain there is love in fountain. Only this way you help Master. Only this way you help to effect change in world in way you desire. This is only way, only solution.

Mary: *Right.*

M: Other people with no understanding complexity problem, with no understanding ability Master, ability self these people have different experience. Very different experience but outcome same eventually outcome same. OK? People with no understanding because pain so immense they cannot see beyond pain, cannot think beyond pain, cannot feel beyond pain. Cannot make correct decision for own survival. They become powerless. They become like infant. Only hope for survival for them is to be looked after. They do not have ability help self, they are infant. If infant does not have parent to look after, infant does not survive. More you become like fountain love more you help Master help other, help infant. Must ease pain for people to have different experience. When you have big ice, big ice, like glacier, glacier, little warm, little fire, little sun and glacier become soft, become water. But little little, gentle gentle, this is what fountain love does for pain other. Understand?

Mary: *Yes.*

M: So this is only solution to help world, to help earth to help survival to help vanquish extreme problem. More people become like fountain love, more quickly glacier become soft water.

Mary: *Right.*

M: Love to pain is like sun to ice. And it seem to you because you have so much concern for fellow you think to self how can I be happy when I see so much pain and you feel that you must also suffer. If my fellow beings suffer I must also suffer. What right do I have to be happy when I see so much suffering in the world? What right do I have? But Master explain to you this is the way to help. Only way. Only way. Only way. Most important that you understand this. Then when you happy you must realize what effect you have on other. When you realize effect you have on other, happy become immense because you realize extent of effect. Happy is like the sun and can shine everybody, and so happy inside can shine everyone too. You must not stop to shine because you must be like sun with ice. You serve no one when you think you must suffer also. You make work very difficult for self very difficult for Master, very difficult for fellow. You actually prevent what you seek for other. You have expression. You own worst enemy - this is exactly what you do with this attitude. OK?

Mary: *Yes.*

M: In some society it is admirable to worry other but it has no purpose, only to make more difficult, has no purpose. Must decide and realize effect of attitude. Forget obligation to society. Forget previous teach, what other teach you, forget.

Mary: *Thank you, I understand now.*

M: You have much power, you by self can be such powerful sun and you do not even realize the extent to which you can help other because you have so much power. OK?

Mary: *Thank you Master.*

M: When you realize effect of self sun this make you even more happy because you understand how you help other. Self happy is not only for self. For you this is extremely important and this is exactly the way it is. Happy never for self - always for everybody. Even people not aware Master even people not aware they like sun they understand when they happy, other happy, family happy, friend happy, but for you, not only family, friend but nation, whole nation happy this is extent of power self when sun. OK?

Mary: *Thank you. Master, can I ask another question?*

M: Yes, my dear.

Mary: *You see the concern again the mind setting in, Master says I can get to that stage, but time to us humans is so* *limiting in this lifetime. Is that going to be possible or is it going to be in a future lifetime?*

M: Oh my dear you think Master make life difficult for you? No my dear Master does not show you gift and say you cannot open gift. Of course not. You can begin this immediately, immediately. When you stop to worry other this process happen for you. Master explain you lie quiet, breathe like wind and sun come, happen very quickly for you. You have many idea in head that you do not deserve to be happy, you think other suffer so you must suffer, that other not happy so how can I be happy? This is illusion my dear you must stop this mind to think like this. You give mind proper instruction. Please give mind proper instruction. Master tell you exactly everything so up to you to re-educate mind. Instruct mind. Entirely for you to re-arrange. You do much work for other, now much work for you.

Mary: *Right, is it because I am thinking those kinds of thoughts that my body is suffering? Digestive problems and putting on weight is that also because of my mind?*

M: My dear when think that you do not deserve to be happy, you must suffer – body very obliging. You see nothing make you suffer so body must oblige and make you suffer because mind tells you "you must suffer".

Mary: *Right.*

M: No reason to suffer. Talk to body. Say to body "sun shine inside, every part of body can lie in sun" and body very happy.

Mary: *Right.*

M: Body does only what mind tell body to do. OK?

Mary: *OK. But Master I understand I can heal my body that way but I have the most terrible problems with my teeth, it's not something that that I can put right. And that has to be me spending money to fix. There are certain things to tell the mind to manifest and other ways that are more practical ways of healing the body.*

M: When you have mountain, when you have this thing like dynamite then mountain can go whoosh, no more mountain. So when in body many year like this (*Master motions great shaking*), then teeth like mountain collapse. So you very lucky you do not collapse like mountain. You have opportunity to fix teeth but stop to do like this (*motions great shaking again*) - you do not want to collapse like mountain. No reason for dynamite in body. This is what worry do to body.

18 THE ARMY

Mary: *Can you please just remind me again on how to use the army successfully? Maybe I don't believe I can fully command the army and also I don't fully understand what kind of work they can do for me.*

M: OK my dear Master explain to you. You are commander of own mind you must instruct mind to work for benefit self. You must not allow mind to be like vehicle no driver. OK. Mind need driver in control in order to get to destination. Now mind is very capable to do many task, even at same time, like you have computer. You know computer?

Mary: *A little.*

M: Computer is able to do many things at same time so mind also, so you have this suggestion - Master say to you if you imagine you have army this is only mind, this is no separate entity, only mind. Master try to make easy for you to command mind. So you imagine army and you say to army do this, do this, do this, and because army has very good commander, has very good ability to follow order exactly. So you must be very careful with instruction because army do exactly what they are told and once you command army you must realize you must have complete faith and trust in army, they are your faithful servant. You do not have to worry what they do because they undertake instruction precisely, every single instruction. You do not have to worry what they do. They do exactly what you tell them. If this method to control mind is not suitable for you, if it become confuse, then is very easy, do not worry army just say to mind you do what I tell you to do. If you understand army, army is very useful because it help to understand way mind work. For many people mind is mystery but if you say to them mind is like army it become very easy for them to understand. It become very easy for them to instruct army, but if you confuse no problem. Master does not want to confuse. Only important to realize you are commander of mind, commander of army, same thing. Do not allow mind to be like naughty children. If you do not discipline children you have big problem. When children do not have intelligent guidance, life for them become extremely difficult - it is parent job to guide child. It is your job to guide mind.

Mary: *The confusion comes when you are referring to my individual mind or the large whole mind that everyone can draw from.*

M: When Master talk mind is own mind. Only self mind, self-confusion, all problem come from this. When you talk global consciousness no problem. Ah! Master understand, Master understand, Master explain. When you think global consciousness thought from everybody, you see thought everybody and you like aerial and you think you have reception to consciousness everybody and you have confused thought.

Mary: *Yes*.

M: OK Master see problem. You need to distinguish confused thought/own thought - own mind/global mind. For you this is very confusing.

Mary: *Yes*.

M: You receive in your aerial many different information. Yes?

Mary: *Yes*.

M: Some information very comfortable, make you happy, some information disturbing. My dear, problem is created because you believe you must suffer, like other suffer, you look at problem in world and you become very sympathetic. You feel their pain and because you feel their pain you also feel and receive their thought. This is why you receive so much disturbing influence and there is much confuse and uncomfortable in mind. Yes, because you feel is your responsibility to understand these people in order to help these people. OK. So you must remove self, remove concern other in manner that you previously worry. When you find that thought become heavy, thought become unbearable sometime, sometime become unbearable for you?

Mary: *Yes.*

M: Because these are thoughts of many people in pain. When people no love, not necessary for you to immerse self, this is damage for you, much damage for you because to be inside all this pain, all these confused thoughts not necessary for you to understand any pain, not necessary for you to understand thought process other people. Only necessary for you to become like sun. If you take little microscope and look at glacier every little part of glacier with microscope, glacier remain. Glacier does not go away. There is much to see and you have your microscope and you become very cold. No solution, only solution - sun.

Mary: *Yes I understand Master thank you.*

M: Your duty to self and your duty to world is to walk away from other (people's) problem. For you only way to help self and help world. Walk away from other problem. No more reason to suffer, Master does not want you to suffer. Because you have power Master wants you to have sun. Master wants you to help Master, wants you to shine sun everybody. OK. Please do not suffer.

Mary: *I don't want to suffer.*

M: But you choose.

Mary: *I am not conscious that I choose.*

M: You must be vigilant commander then. Be very vigilant.

19 PLAN FOR SUCCESS

M: Master explain to you - when you understand simplicity – complex become perfect. Perfect complexity understand? So you understand simplicity and complex become perfect. Simplicity and complexity together, OK?

Mary: *Yes.*

M: When you do work for world it will be ...it will be....events will reach very far, be like a big net, so in order for project to be success net must be perfect geometry, like geometry perfect, so when you look you see how much beauty in structure, much order in structure and every single aspect of plan, every single aspect of plan operate precisely, perfectly with maximum benefit to other, understand? But first must examine small, must examine seed, must examine seed. If seed become damage, plant become damage, same with plan very complex, always must pay attention more than most people deem necessary - to seed, to detail. When detail at formation is considered, every single detail, then success inevitable. Not only success inevitable but consequence benefit other. Not just for you success, but for all people. So when other in great hurry to progress plan you must say to them, "Wait we must make sure preparation correct so no possibility for damage plant." Other is in great hurry, great hurry, but like man who try to run with rope on leg, fall over, and does not run very far before he fall over. But because you pay attention to detail you see rope on leg, he does not see rope on leg. This is example, only example. So is OK, because is balance. You have this dynamic energy, energy wanting to explode, to create, so when you make sure seed perfect then other come with dynamic energy and then grow like magic because you have perfect seed and you have dynamic energy, in combination you have rapid growth, success assured. Understand? (Clapping) Master like pupil, good pupil understand everything. Understand everything. You have other question?

Mary: *I have a lot of questions, Master and thank you very much for coming through.*

M: Must prioritize question. Because if too many question then you forget most important question.

Mary: *The most important question for me is that I really need to know and understand. You say I am a good pupil, but when you are talking about a seed you are talking about something I am going to do in the future?*

M: My dear this apply to every situation, this is fundamental law for success. But at moment you have comrade who has much energy and project to do something very enormous and Master explain to you for success you must examine every minute detail at very beginning so seed perfect and whole, not even plant, whole enormous tree perfect, but this apply every situation, no exception.

Mary: *Because there are so many changes coming in my life, where I am moving, as you say there is a project that I am handling at the moment that could be very good for me, and Master says that I am in the right place now and that I just need to apply the attention to detail to whatever comes.*

M: Yes my dear and when many opportunities come to you, you examine each one and if you do not see perfect, then you let go, do not even consider to fix, because many people have proposition for you but you say, half-bake, many half-bake and it is not in your best interest to try to fix when someone come to you with proposition it must be perfect. So you examine detail but you do not try to fix. If perfect then you consider. Much energy lost when half bake because you see project and plan half-bake but you must understand person who present this to you also half bake - you cannot fix understand? *(Half-baked is an expression in the UK of someone who is ungrounded and impractical, even slightly "crazy")*

You must look at plan and you look at person together, one give other clue for you, if you unsure look at people, if they appear to have problem to be half-bake, plan half-bake. So you look both to help understand, to help decision, but also when something presents to you is perfect then there is no hesitation because you see perfection and body sing. Body sing because body recognize perfection.

So when you see plan and for you it does not look perfect, for you half-bake, the same also apply for you. You see theory, you listen explanation and it doesn't seem perfect for you - so don't listen, it is of no consequence, everyone has own path, OK? Do not concern other people path. OK? It is necessary to have many different path. If you have whole world try to walk in road, road not big enough.

Mary: *It's probably a similar question because that is a huge thing in the world at the moment. What they say is, people from other planets are busy assisting us, like the space brothers, is it another aspect again of mind trying to reconcile what is happening?*

M: When you have different language, speak different word same thing. Understand? So same. Do not concern self. There are many like Master who help, many like Master.

Mary: *That's where my confusion happens because there are people out there that say certain ascended Masters are speaking and they express who they are and what their names are, how people understand the.... Is Master speaking through Alison as the voice of God. I am asking very clearly now, whatever connects us to the holy source is this who is speaking to me at the moment?*

M: You must understand, this topic complex, to understand whole, to understand complete must also be complete. When you have understanding - but not mind understanding - then you know everything. But for mind to understand complete is not possible because mind can only function as far with what you call theory, idea, try to analyze, try to make complete fit into very small understanding and because this is not possible this is why mind create so many possibility. Because this possibility is like this (*motions small*) complete like this (*motions huge*) it does not work 100% because you will never understand with mind, so mind think must be this, must be this, must be this. Not possible to understand with mind. So forget mind and when you are able to escape mind then you have experience of complete, total understanding, all knowledge become available to you, not even available because you become same. There is no separate you from experience and knowledge, no separation, you become experience, you become knowledge, there is no separation. So when you try to understand with mind, year after year, after year, after year, after year, but problem mind is never happy with solution. Mind believe it can find solution so it create more, create more, create more, create more. Mind become very busy.

And this is directly in opposition to understanding with no separation. Busy mind, is crazy mind, is like you ask someone direction, you want to find something and they say Oh yes I know, but you do not realize this is not their home and they send you over there and you go over there and you lost so you ask someone else and they say I know where you want to go and off you go and you do this many, many, many time and you never stop to question these people. How do they know which direction for me to go? Only one person know which direction for me to go. Self, and what you call God, what you call Divine, what you understand as supreme power, but is only your understanding but is sufficient for you to allow to guide you, is sufficient even though understanding is inaccurate and can never be accurate until you escape mind, is sufficient to lead you in direction away from being lost. OK? Mind never satisfied.

20 BECOME THE COMMANDER OF YOUR MIND

M: Mind is like any tool. You have tool, any tool in world, every single tool you can use for benefit, you can use for destruction. Same mind. Learn to use mind for benefit. Learn to control mind. Imagine you hold some scissor and scissor have mind of own and scissor go crazy. Does not only cut what you want - it cut everything. This is not good situation, as you direct hand to have control over scissor so you must direct self to have control over mind, determine for self usefulness of mind and uselessness, not even useless but destructive mind. Is in your control, is only tool. Mind is not there to control you, you must control mind. You are not your mind, you can control mind.

Mary: *I don't want to work through the mind anymore and I know you said to do the breathing exercises, but I am really finding it ………*

M: Mind is tool to discern to use for benefit. Do not say you do not want to use mind, you do not want to be zombie! You must be very careful what you say. It is same, you examine seed, you examine detail everything, then you will get perfection. So when you separate and control mind then it become easy for you to escape mind. You are in control of mind, it is very easy to escape mind. Because already when you in control of mind already there is separation because mind does not control you. You control mind - beginning of separation, beginning of realization of self because you see self is not mind. Understand?

So must examine mind, control mind, decide function mind, decide work you wish mind to do for self because mind is tool, and you must become master of your mind and direct mind. You make rule - you make decision for mind. You become master of mind.

Mary: *And how can I master the mind?*

M: You examine detail! You look at how mind work. You look at conversation in head. Many conversation in head huh? Many conversation in head and you resolve to lessen and increase. You increase for benefit and you lessen just by intention to do, to look, to listen - to have conversation and listen to conversation and then say to mind "This does not serve me you are my tool to help, you are here to serve, here to help. This conversation does not help". Mind will do what you tell mind to do. If you do not tell mind what to do mind will run like crazy scissor. Mind is tool, when you understand this and you give direction, you give instruction. You remember army? You must give direction and give instruction to mind also. You are General, you are Commander. So many people have this wonderful tool, they have a mind, the most wonderful tool in existence for them. It is a tool - they do not even realize what they have. You have everything my dear, you have everything. The most wondrous tool in sight. This mind which so many people say cause so many problem only because they do not use tool. They like child with tool they do not even understand. You do not give scissor to child but people like child with mind. OK?

Mary: *May I ask a question about the work Alison wants to do about the wonderful book she is inspired to write to help people, will it be...*

[Master's laughter fills the room!]

M: *This one* has same problem, she does not use mind. Also same problem my dear. Also same problem. You will see much change because she listen Master. She listen Master, and Master be very close *this one* all time. Very close all time. So all *this one* need to do is live like Master. You have finished questions?

Mary: *I have many questions but now the most important thing is how I can get Master to be close to me to find myself fully?*

M: Self is not lost, no need to find self, need to examine mind. Need to command mind like General, make mind work for self. If you believe self lost then mind in control, self not lost. Self needs to remember self is General, is Commander of mind. Mind is tool. Self not lost, self forget power. You see my dear, can you imagine to have this knowledge that self has power over mind and when there is no discernment and there is corruption of people they use this information to become dominant over fellow. But you all have this capability, not one single person more capable than another. Not one. Only some realize power, understand how to use mind and make other believe they have no power, every single one has same capability. Do not let other fool self. Do not believe self lost. Is illusion, and mind become out of control because self does not control. Only reason why mind is out of control is because self does not realize own power, does not realize self is General self is Commander of own army. Do not believe when people Say "Oh yes I know - go there, go there, go there". Then you become lost, you become confused. Even you can lose life because you can spend every day follow direction, follow direction.

Mary: *Why do we forget self and allow mind to control us?*

M: Because when you very small child you were told you have no power, you are not allowed power, parent teach, society teach, communication world teach. So everybody believe lie, no one question, everybody accept they have no power and this is very convenient for certain people, people who know otherwise, do not readily want to tell you, do not readily want to dispel illusion.

Mary: *Are you saying we are all responsible for the entire mess this world is in for misunderstanding mind?*

M: It is for individual to correct; only individual can correct. And it is for people with supreme knowledge to make information available to other so they understand problem, then they understand own power, understand own capability. It is necessary for people with supreme knowledge to help other and then it become individual responsibility to help self but at moment information available does not speak correct information.

Mary: *Master isn't that why we have this truth coming through so people can be given the right information and helped?*

M: My dear already happen, it happen. It happen at moment. You understand completely? When you make change in self you become like beacon to other. You do not have to say to other "Oh yes I know which way for you to go".

You do not do this. Only become beacon. Do not direct. Do not become same like, direct here, direct here, only become beacon, because power become immense - capability is limitless, this is how change happen when you become beacon. You see, when you understand mind little and you feel and sense self and feel and sense mind and self become separate, experience of self grow, mind is not in charge, mind is not dominant. Experience of self become dominant. Experience of self is like beacon. Even at this moment you feel self become more luminescent. When you have beacon and you feel luminescent you cannot help but influence other because they bathe in your light and just to bathe in your light for them is like to drink water when you in desert.

There is so much work for you to do and if you are not in control of your mind how can you do this work. There is so much for you to do because you have chosen to do so and are capable to do so.

21 BEING MINDFUL

Gemma: *Is there anything I need to do? Basically, can Master tell me how I can be more conscious?*

M: You explain understanding conscious. Question not clear for self.

Gemma: *How do I remain conscious from moment to moment and not lapse. Can you give me an exercise?*

M: Even this question not clear, you do not sleep? Be more clear. Be more clear.

Gemma: *Mindful. How to be mindful at all times. Be mindful of my actions.*

M: My dear, my dear, my dear, you have understanding incorrect for experience self. You hear other talk talk talk talk, and you believe they know. But they create error, and because error you look in place empty. Futile search, because you receive inadequate instruction.

This is problem, so do not struggle. Struggle not necessary. This is big error. Big error. Do not need to give mind so much attention. You say to mind to behave - do not be like naughty children. Do not want to sit and look at naughty children! This is why when somebody says to you – "Be mindful - look at mind." and you look at naughty children. This is very confuse.

Gemma: *Yes*.

M: Very confuse. Does not help self. Must say to mind: **"Behave self! Do not be like naughty children. I do not want to look at naughty children".**

This is first error, because if you look at naughty children, children always naughty. Very happy for you to look, even they perform more! Understand? So first step - mind behave.

You say to mind : **"From now on I control you. You do not control me, you behave!"**

This is first step. You stop to listen other, because they have misunderstanding. They have inability to communicate wisdom. Listen Master. Master direction like rocket. Like rocket. Other direction not even like snail. Snail move very slow, other direction does not even move.

Gemma: *Can I ask, on a practical level, if what I am doing with a charity, for instance a business, can you give me any guidance if I am doing the right thing or where I should be going with this charity, or how I can best serve the charity?*

M: When you have the ability to control mind, you have ability to discern right for you every situation. You say to mind, you instruct mind, to create situation for best serve other best serve self. You tell mind to do work for you to create this situation.

Gemma: *I think I understand. Do you mean I don't need to focus on charity, but need to focus on mind?*

M: First step mind, then mind provide accurate scenario for self, for other. Only requirement. If mind is like naughty children then calamity, any situation calamity, every situation can be calamity with naughty children. So when you understand to control mind, give proper instruction - every situation perfection

Gemma: *It is very difficult to control mind.*

M: But you are Commander! Only need to give instruction. Very simple. If you believe difficult - very difficult. Only necessary to become Commander. If you have naughty children, naughty children kick leg - you say "STOP KICK LEG!" This is simple my dear, this is simple, same, same. Do not make complicate. Do not make complicate. Mind likes complicate – this is naughty children.

Gemma: *Of course, so just, you say, keep simple.*

M: Yes my dear, keep simple because solution always simple. Always simple.

Gemma: *Yes, yes.*

M: When you remember naughty children kick leg - then you remember you are Commander.

Gemma: *Of course.*

M: And you remember simple instruction. This is not difficult.

Gemma: *Sometimes it seems very difficult.*

M: Again same answer.

Gemma: *Of course, so I just need to keep doing what I am doing.*

M: You need article to remind self, naughty children. Like people have knot handkerchief, you need article. So you must find article. Something to remind self naughty children

Gemma: *What kind of article?*

M: You find something make you very angry children; something, just even little to look with eye. Something like this in pocket, so always remind self - even attach to key.

(Master motions drawing a small square in the air to suggest a picture)

Gemma: *Oh, OK.*

M: Even attach to key - remind self every time. Never forget.

Gemma: *Very simple. Thank you.*

M: Yes my dear when you remember naughty children kick leg then you laugh at mind.

Gemma: *Yes, of course.*

M: Mind think mind clever but you more clever.

G: *I think so; I will start to believe so. Yes thank you Master.*

M: When you realize, you clever and you control mind you have ability immense.

Gemma: Yes.

M: At moment you not realize possibility.

22 MEDITATION

Mary: *So Master, all the experiences we have on a daily basis is all created by the mind?*

M: Is not simple question. If mind is still, very quiet, life still happen. Life still happen, for experience life very different, experience love, you experience happy. So when mind very busy - experience very different. Life does not disappear when mind become quiet. Experience change. So, mind create experience, does not create life, create experience of life. Mind create situation because experience is created by mind. Action also from mind, so in this respect you create life for self, but when you make mind very quiet, experience (of) life very pleasant. Action become expression of love - is alternative experience. Understand? Is this sufficient explanation?

Mary: *The key here is to have a still mind. This problem, for me and for most people, is how to still the mind. Why is the mind in control of everything - it becomes master.*

M: Because you do not control mind. It is possible to control mind. To give attention to something other than mind, but you give attention to mind.

Mary: *OK. So where does the attention need to go?*

M: There is a space. And Master make you feel space. Purpose of meditation is to train self to find space. Within this space is very easy to exclude mind. When you find space you understand process. Enter into this space, then you will have complete command of mind. Mind become instrument for you and you are not servant of mind.

Mary: *Thank you Master.*

M: If you imagine atoms and when atoms very dense, then you cannot move. So imagine around body, inside body, imagine when you breathe atom become very fluid, no more dense. Atom become so fluid then atom become very separate and there is enormous space in between atom, find this space, reside in this space. You can use this. Even you can use your mind to help you find this space, because, mind can visualize atom - so you can use mind to make atom fluid. You can say to mind *"Separate these atoms so I can see space in between atom"* and mind will oblige because you have given something for mind to do. Then you can trick mind because you find space. In this space there is no mind. So while mind is busy make atom separate, you can trick mind and enter space. And you can use breathe to separate atom also. Like when you blow leaf, leaf blow away in wind, so when you breathe you imagine breath send atom away and leave space. Very interesting exercise for you. Very significant exercise for you.

Note: On another day Mary returned to the question of meditation:

Mary: *Can I ask some questions Master? Master said very clearly that I needed to do a specific type of meditation and that I needed to do relaxation and breathing. I am finding it very difficult for my mind to let Master come through.*

M: My dear you must realize that when you do this practice Master does not enter immediately. Always one step, one step. Always process, do not even look for Master. If you look for Master immediately, you forget one step one step OK? If you on edge of cliff big chasm, you cannot jump to other side. You look to other side but you forget to look at bridge, you do not even see bridge so you do not walk bridge, you look chasm and you think I cannot get to other side, Master is on other side. OK? Do not look to Master, find bridge and you walk very easy. So even do not look for bridge. But when you stop to look (*cease looking*) for Master, bridge appear. You understand?

Mary: *To tell you the truth Master no. I must be stupid.*

M: Do not worry you not stupid my dear, you have wonderful mind you have excellent understanding. Master will explain more for you. Sometimes people understand chasm, sometimes understand bridge, but for you, you need different explanation only for this reason. OK, you become very still, you concentrate breath, you close eye, and then mind look for Master. You say to self I become very still, I concentrate breath, I close eye and you do not know what to do next. Your mind instructs to think that you do something incorrect. OK, because you do not have experience so you think you do something incorrect. Only reason because you expect - so you must not expect, you must wait very patient, very patient. If you lie down in field, only person in field, very quiet very still. Some cloud in sky. You love sun but you see cloud in sky. OK, and you know from experience you just lay very still and cloud very slow move and you see sun. Understand?

Mary: *Yes.*

M: Same, same like this. Same like this. When you lie very still even may seem to you very slow, but cloud disappear and you see sun and Master is sun. When you see cloud in sky you do not worry where is sun you wait very patient. OK?

Mary: *Yes Master, thank you.*

M: This is same. Do not look for Master, realize Master is sun, breathe is wind, breathe is wind, wind blow cloud so sun come. Understand? Breathe is wind, wind blow cloud away and sun come. More consistent breathe more cloud go away.

Mary: *I understand Master, thank you.*

M: And when you breath, [*breathes in deeply*] like this you bring power into body. When you breathe like this (*breathes out*) wind blow away cloud. Power take away dark from mind, from body. You breathe in power; you move like this, you move cloud. Need more explanation? OK. OK. Very easy. Yes?

Mary: *I can experience that little bit of sunshine coming and I really want to experience more than the mind, what it is like* *to experience the sun. Is there something I can do on a daily basis, maybe a little ritual maybe the way I approach to be in that right space to bring myself closer to clarity? Perhaps the way I should meditate, because I was told that I should be facing towards the East when I meditate? Is there a ritual I can follow to make that possible?*

M: You must examine thought. When you say to Master is there something for me to do to bring me closer - there is no distance, there is no closer. Just to think you need to be closer you create situation, you create distance. There is no distance; there is no distance my dear. When people think they have to find something and they go on treasure hunt, but the thing they search for is not lost, is not lost. This is futile treasure hunt. So when you sit to do meditation you sit to enjoy self, you do not sit to search something. You sit to enjoy self.

Marie: *I have one question. I sit every day and meditate, but I don't have a clear line to upstairs. Why?*

M: What do you expect when you meditate?

Marie: To *have a connection to source.*

M: Yes my dear, describe this connection.

Marie: *Knowledge, wisdom, but I don't seem to hear anything. I hear in the middle of the night but not when I meditate.*

M: So you want to talk Master, when *you* want to talk to Master Huh?

Marie: *Yes.*

M: Maybe this is problem.

Marie: *I should sit schtum (quiet) and expect whatever happens?*

M: You see my dear when you are ready to receive you will receive. OK?

Marie: *What do I have to do to receive?*

M: You already do receive, but at time does not suit you. You already have knowledge, you already have wisdom.

Marie: *Thank you. It's just that I have friends that tell me about the amazing things that they get when they meditate in the mornings, but that never seems to happen to me.*

M: This is not a problem, not a problem my dear. Many year you very busy in mornings, you, for reason you do things when your body wants to do things so time for you different, time for you different...

Marie: *Thank you, I understand.*

M: When you decide how you would like Master to come, you do not see when Master comes because you look other way.

Marie: *OK, thank you I understand.*

M: Do not try to be like other people my dear, only can be like self. People tell you many things please do not listen, please do not listen other people. You very wise, have much knowledge, listen self. Other people tell you do this, do that, come here, go there, you know exactly what you want but listen too many other people. You think for some reason, my dear, other people know better,

Marie: *Because I have always felt that I came in through the back door and not through the front door and just never felt good enough spiritually.*

M: Nobody better than you, not one, not one better than you.

Marie: *OK, thank you.*

M: You must remember. You talk diamonds. People have diamonds inside. My dear you are diamond mine. So where else to look? Nowhere else to look, too many diamonds to look at in self.

Marie: *I understand.*

M: Why do you think so many people come to you? Huh?

Marie: *I don't have the answer to that.*

M: They see the diamond mine. Even you don't see, they see.

Marie: *OK thank you Master.*

Mary: *We were discussing earlier, how people will be taught to receive what Alison is receiving. Will it be different for everyone?*

M: Result same, even process same, but journey different. Understand?

Mary: *OK. The journey may be different but the way people will be receiving you will be the same way?*

M: Yes my dear. When you talk Master you get knowledge because Master talk to you.

Rachel: *Can anybody do that through meditation?*

M: So many people have many strange idea when they meditate. They have idea of meditation instead of allowing Master in, so this is one problem, but meditation very good way, bit slow, but very good way.

Rachel: *What is a quick way?*

M: Sing! Singing very good way to clear so energy is more conducive for Master to enter. OK. When you vibrate very different so Master can come very similar vibration, then you feel Master.

Mary: *So are you saying that if I am terribly sad and I am crying then you can't come in?*

M: Very difficult my dear, very difficult, Master try help you but it's like you hide under blanket, you hide because a little self-indulgent.

Mary: *Thank you Master I understand. So the vibrations have to be right before you can actually enter. So how does a person perceive you because now you are speaking through Alison how would I know, would I be able to hear your voice in my head, to know this, to be able to feel you coming into my body?*

M: My dear when Master come you know. No questions, you know when Master come. For you there will be much light, be like golden sun in head and body, almost like you say blinded and this will take your attention from the mind enough so that Master come in.

Mary: *Thank you.*

M: Different everybody. Different everybody. Master always find quick way. Not same everybody... Much light for you so mind, even less than one second, will stop and Master come. OK?

Mary: *Thank you.*

Master gives Mary experience of energy of oneness.

23 EARTH – RESSURECTION OR DESTRUCTION?

M: Welcome, welcome my dear.

Mary: *Welcome, thank you for coming. We have many questions.*

M: One moment, Master want to clarify situation world. At moment is like chicken run, chicken with no head. You have expression? Chicken no head, run run run! People like this very crazy at moment. But chicken have limited intelligence. This is same people, run like chicken - very limited understanding. If they have understanding, they do not run like chicken no head. (laughs) OK? So always they believe they know everything. Suddenly, they find their world, as they perceive world, collapse. For them this is big catastrophe and they do not understand because for many year they think they know everything. They think no one can disturb life, no one can cause upheaval because they construct life for them perfect, for other - destruction. They do not see problem - to make life perfect for them they cause destruction (for) other. They do not even contemplate effect on other. This is not perfection, to believe perfection this is illusion – this is why so much catastrophe at moment, because they cause so much destruction. Eventually perfect even destroy. So what use this knowledge? What use this attitude? And when perfect collapse they run like headless chicken. But they create collapse because whole perception - complete illusion; no consideration for other. Only way for resurrection world is to consider every individual without exception, no exception. You have questions my dear?

Mary: *Yes thank you Master. Thank you for what you said about what's going on in the world today. There is the fear that because of natural catastrophes the planet may be annihilated or the natural catastrophes will bring an imbalance which will kill a majority of the population. This is the kind of knowledge that is being spread around in the world and I wanted some comfort from you, some explanation as to that Master.*

M: You worry annihilation?

Mary: *Yes.*

M: Complete destruction everything? This is, this is possible, but is not imminent.

Mary: *Right.*

M: There is much to do before conditions allow such event. Many people scaremonger. Also many people aware necessary adjustment and work very hard to create necessary adjustment so between situation presently observed and complete annihilation is much in between, much in between, do not worry. This event is extremely unlikely, extremely, although possible, very possible, but at moment is very distant. Very distant. Do not worry.

Mary: *Thank you Master. There is a lot being said at the moment about certain what are perceived as spaceships within our solar system apparently that are mopping up radiation and controlling the environment of the earth. What does Master have to say about that?*

M: There is confusion; there is confusion in mind other. There is intervention, and help. When people talk spaceship - is very infantile description but they do not understand process. When they observe intervention they never experience other reality, so they mold experience into something similar for understanding. Understand?

Mary: *OK, so the mind creates all that in order to understand.*

M: But intervention happen, help come, definitely help come. Is necessary, because calamity needs to be avoided. Help come. But not spaceship, is only, is only small error. But sometimes, when people believe error it make confusion; it detract from complete understanding because you believe spaceship, then mind create other scenario, because already spaceship then - little green men even! Understand? So small error can become big error. So at moment small error, because mind is very infantile, in relation to magnificent process. Is sufficient to realize help come, this is sufficient. When you try to be very specific because mind require explanation, mind require to fit experience unusual into previous experience, to enable understanding – is not possible, is not possible. So then mind create story.

Mary: *Yes, right.*

M: Story serve mind - but create barrier, and prevent understanding because mind create illusion, create story. Does not allow self to have complete experience because mind make you distracted. Understand? Only know help happen. Is sufficient. When you have this perspective - more help come. <u>More</u> help come. Mind create barrier. Because mind create story, is barrier to help. Do not imagine spaceship, do not imagine little green men. Only know help come, then you be like magnet for help. Help come, is sufficient. Very important not to create barrier. Many story prevent help come, many story prevent help come, and is very intentional others. This is intention of other to prevent help come. OK?

Mary: *Thank you Master, just I understand, because you have said that you have a plan, and I have complete trust that you know exactly what is going on, but when you refer to other as if there is an opposing force that wants to prevent the help from coming do I even need to look at what that opposing force is?*

M: No my dear, no my dear this is very dangerous for whole process.

Mary: *No looking?*

M: No my dear, must focus on help come. Be magnet for help come.

Mary: Complete trust in Master.

M: Complete trust process! Complete trust process. Do not listen story. Do not create story. Explain other, do not create story. Explain process. Very important.

Mary: *Could you please remind me on process as I need to open myself to Master.*

M: Explain my dear? Master confuse question. You want explanation process help come?

Mary: *Yes, are you saying just trust in the process? Because when you said to explain to others that there is a process ….*

M: Yes my dear Master explain to you already, thought/mind create barrier because mind create story. This is barrier, this prevent outcome, when you remove story and you understand help come, this is only requirement, very important for clarification other people. This process come. Very simple, do not obstruct with story, do not obstruct with mind, understand, because very simple to explain because very simple process, mind does not like simple. So mind says Master explain, explain, explain. This is mind, mind likes to confuse.

24 *RITUAL*

Rick: *I have a question about the importance of ritual in churches and temples. Does it matter if someone does ritual?*

M: When ritual is performed with understanding, with appreciation for ritual and understanding significance - immense power. When ritual perform like robot little power, but with appreciation with understanding, immense power. But many people do not understand importance ritual. They try to emulate other, try to find power other but they make error because they would have more benefit to look for self, self-knowledge, self-expression. Expression self-love. They try to emulate.

Rick: *Does a self-realized person need to do ritual?*

M: Is not necessary but is like sun on face. It increase pleasure. It increase pleasure for other.

Rick: *Thank you.*

M: When you do ritual, imagine artefact. Sometimes you use artifact. Imagine like magnifying glass, when sun come and sun make power. Understand? When you do ritual for self realize sun come, include sun in ritual realize artifact is magnifying glass, more powerful, more sun. When sun come through artifact, it reflect back to self and self become more like sun.

25 HONORING ANCESTORS

M: Welcome my dear.

Mary: *Thank you being here Master. We wanted to know if you could talk to us about the importance of honoring the memory of our ancestors.*

M: Explain Master self-understanding first.

Mary: *Explain?*

M: Explain self. You have understanding ancestor, no understanding?

Mary: *What I perceive as ancestors are the people through whom I came, parents, grandparents, great-grandparents and so on. The physical lineage I guess.*

M: Explain understanding significance. You ask Master explain significance Master ask explain self-understanding ancestors.

Mary: *I really don't know.*

M: You have no understanding? This is what Master ask. Ancestor very important because no ancestor - nobody. No ancestors, nothing. No ancestor, no *this one*, no this one, no this one. Is like atomic bomb in whole world not one survivor. No ancestor same as atomic bomb. This is importance of ancestor. People forget importance of ancestor. Ancestor struggle, much struggle, many ancestor. You believe you struggle, sometimes you struggle. Ancestors more struggle! 1000 time more struggle! Ancestors' life always more difficult. Have to work very hard to maintain environment, maintain knowledge, maintain lineage. Understand lineage? So Master explain, ancestor work very hard - more hard self. So when you acknowledge and appreciate ancestor, is like when you recognize child. Child always try very hard for approval parent and, when parent give approval child, child become very happy, same ancestor. When you recognize effort, hardship ancestor, and you appreciate, they become very happy like child and when ancestor very happy - self very happy; because ancestor is foundation for self. Remember no separation, no separation. You do not make car shiny on outside, clean and shiny on outside and allow to deteriorate inside, you also maintain inside vehicle, not just outer appearance. Engine work very hard – must maintain engine. Understand? Same self, very important for you to make self shiny, clean, look beautiful. So remember, ancestor like engine, work very hard, need to maintain, need to recognize – engine make car move; provide power for car, same ancestor self. When you recognize ancestor, when you maintain engine - car very powerful. Very powerful. Very powerful ancestor.

Mary: *Thank you Master. So how can we honor and appreciate ancestors and show how we feel?*

M: Same like child. You communicate child pleasure, you communicate child appreciation existence. Same ancestor. Very simple. Even one thought, one day, ancestor – very simple.

Mary: *Let me clarify. To me ancestors mean physical ancestors, my physical ancestors and I am the product of that. So how can they connect, how can they be one? Can they be in the spirit world and I have to be aware of them?*

M: Already connection – do not have to worry how to connect, already connection -separation illusion.

Mary: *Right. Then can you please clarify, did all people today have a common ancestor or were there many ancestors when the different lineages developed?*

M: OK my dear, before ancestor, no separation, no substance, no substance. Master communicate to you to experience before substance. This is only way to explain. Only when you transcend experience physical body, when you experience self, only then will you begin understanding. BEGIN understanding! And begin experience before substance. Only then. Mind is not capable to dissect information, to arrive at experience before substance. Incapable for mind because mind is product of creation and you require experience previous to substance.

Mary: *Exactly.*

M: So my dear, little waiting, little waiting to transcend physical experience. At moment not possible. At moment you must honor ancestors, create condition, for experience previous substance. First must honor ancestor – this is one step, one step. When you understand one step you understand other. One step one step – you do not have capability to comprehend and if mind become entrenched in more theory this is obstruction.

Mary: *Right.*

M: So one step, one step for you – for everybody. Ultimately, understanding is product of experience and then there is no error. If mind were capable to understand. IF mind were capable to understand with explanation there would be so many errors. Understand? Only way is experience, and understanding become product of experience.

Mary: *OK, so Master we are going back to the fact that the mind needs to be clear.*

M: Mind needs to understand theory and to understand experience. If belief is flawed, is problem. So need correction. When Master talk, Master always direct mind and illustrate error so mind has less work to do. This is method Master. When mind is less busy, because mind create so much work, when mind is less busy, more easy to find self, then when you experience self, have complete understanding and mind become like a new companion. Like a companion. At moment for many people mind is a nuisance. When you experience self, understand everything, mind become companion. Very different experience. At moment mind display like child has tantrum. This is not nature of child. When child is unhappy child display tantrum, this is same mind many people, and they do not realize this is not nature of mind. This is unhappy mind. They do not consider mind to be anything other than like child with tantrum because they only see tantrum.

Mary: *Right.*

M: Mind is waiting for love. Mind is waiting for love.

Mary: *Master.*

M: Yes my dear.

Mary: *The vast majority of people believe that God, the creator or whatever you like to call it, created one man and one woman, Adam and Eve, and that we all came through their lineage and I am one of them because that is what I was brought up in. So how am I to understand the ancestors? Am I just to understand that that is a fact?*

M: When you honor ancestor you do not have to specify ancestors, too many ancestors! Cannot identify a million ancestors. Ha ha ha! This will send you crazy. Must only *honor* ancestors. Ancestors as collective ancestor. Do not have to identify individual ancestors. Mother Father very easy. Grandmother Grandfather very easy; but if you go beyond several generation this is enormous task and you say to Master "How do I honor every ancestor right back to creation, to moment substance appear?" This is impossible, impossible, and Master say to you when you honor ancestor, when you eventually remove experience physical body and experience self, you have complete understanding, complete knowledge, all question answered. This is best way, because if Master say to you explanation, mind start to think and analyze explanation. Other begin to analyze explanation. This create many problem. This does not serve purpose to find self. This create more problem. This is counter-productive. When you listen Master, when you experience self, you understand everything, have complete knowledge, this is your desire.

Mary: *Yes.*

M: And this is desire Master for everybody. Master does not want to confuse, does not want to create more confusion for many minds. OK? So - meditation – enjoy self, do not look for self, self is. If you imagine a lotus flower, lotus flower beautiful, lotus flower has very extending root, root go down into murky water and produce beautiful lotus flower. Root is ancestor.

26 CONFUSED ABOUT CONFUSION

Rachel: *You say with the confusion, when I look back and sometimes think I have been confused and at the time I didn't feel it as confusion. I think a lot of people are feeling a difference and when I look at my patients a lot of them are feeling confusion but they don't class it as confusion, but they feel it as fear, can you give me more clarity on what this confusion is - because I am confused about this.*

M: OK. There is confusion and there is fear also but always where there is confusion people try to find reason. Then they find reason and they become afraid. So confusion can create fear because they do not understand, so they become frightened. So underneath fear, if you look underneath fear you can find confusion.

Rachel: *And does worry cause confusion.*

M: Worry only fear. Fear of something. Confusion because people feel problem (of) everybody.

Rachel: *OK so they feel overwhelmed?*

M: They like aerial, like aerial they pick signal, become confused.

Mary: *Why is that happening now?*

M: This because we must learn to disperse confusion, disperse problem together. Whenever problem arise solution is found. Whenever there is problem people look for solution. OK so, problem confusion, but also confusion because problem many people. Master confuse you?

[Laughter]

Rachel: *I'm dispersing.*

Rob: *So the problem causes confusion which causes problem which causes more confusion so it's a circle.*

M: But Master tell you solution stop confusion.

Rachel: *So do we disperse the confusion by just loving, by accepting what is and not accepting anything as a problem?*

M: Way to disperse is to understand confusion pass through you like wind. When you feel confusion even just to realize this is just wind passing through it will go. Do not have to do anything, very simple, do not have to do...

Rachel: *Nothing.*

M: Exactly, exactly - you learning!

Rachel: *Slowly.*

M: Very quickly my dear, many people learn nothing.

Rachel: *I am very confused in my acupuncture practice so now I know why so now I can just blow it away.*

M: Yes you find reason confusion. Confusion nothing to do acupuncture.

Rachel: *Yes it's just the outside aerial.*

M: Yes my dear. OK. Many people confuse many things, but, all same problem - they become aerial everybody. Because so many problem in world they feel everything but they cannot separate, they cannot identify problem so it become confusion.

Rachel: *So it's like a mass consciousness is running away with itself.*

M: No running away with itself, no but,

Rachel: *Panicking?*

M: But like rabbit run many different direction, no clear direction, signal become not like music, but like noise. Understand? Understand? Like that. When people have much understanding each other, when they work together and love each other, then they can make music together; but when they do not act like this then it's like noise, nothing understood, just confusion.

Rachel: *So what do we say to people to stop them being confused? Because you said before it's unwise to talk about* *what we have learned because it confuses people – they have their own path step by step. So what advice can we give to people? Shall we just be the tree for them?*

M: No my dear, this very simple message you can tell everybody. This one very simple. People understand. People understand this one.

Rachel: *OK*

M: Very simple.

Rachel: *So what they are feeling isn't just their problem it's the whole of society then.*

M: Whole world, whole world. When they become like tree and wind pass through they feel better just by understanding this process, by understanding this is not their confusion just for them. You see, if you hear your neighbor make big, big noise many, many time and if you think this noise in head, you go crazy. When you realize this noise someone else you do not go crazy. Understand. So when you understand confusion not yours you stop being confused. Same thing.

You see, if people do not stop confused, they lose control, they will go crazy.

Mary: *Master, maybe I am lacking understanding here, but the confusion in the world is intensifying now, is that to bring us into that unity to make us feel as one entity?*

M: Yes my dear, the only way to disperse confusion is for everybody to become like tree. So we must all become like tree. Everybody feel everything.

Mary: *How do we get that message across to people quickly?*

Rachel: *Because they will think we are crazy if we say go and understand a tree.*

M: Master explain you, very simple. You understand everything Master says?

Rachel: *Yes. That they are ...*

M: So you explain exactly same way. If you understand Master, other people understand you. You do not have to change, very simple way. You find people not stupid, they understand. They need this knowledge like they need water.

Rachel: *Anyone that has ever mentioned trees before in our society is usually regarded as crazy, nuts. Um, it's not that they are not clever, I'm wondering if they will get past the...um, I don't know ...*

Rob: *There are some people that do criticize, they are not ready to understand.*

Rachel: *There are tree huggers, they laugh at you.*

M: My dear this is metaphor. Master did not say hug tree Master say ...

Rachel: *No, but that's what people who hug trees are called.*

M: You create problem. There is no problem. You create confusion.

[Laughter]

Rachel: *OK.*

Mary: *In the world today all you hear people talking about is big issues, like there is an oil crisis and there is a food crisis and there are money problems. How do you get people to draw away from this whole crisis situation? They do believe that we are heading for a major catastrophe worldwide.*

M: Yes my dear.

Mary: *How do we diffuse that?*

M: Master just explain. Master just explain.

Mary: *So is this just illusion.*

M: This is all confusion. This is what happen, confusion accelerate, people lose control.

Mary: *It's the origin of the confusion that I am concerned for.*

M: Do not worry origin OK? Do not worry origin, this big problem, needs solution. Master tell you solution.

Mary: *Right.*

M: Always when something is problem, then it become very visible OK? So then you fix ... you find solution for this problem. Then you see something else. You only fix what you see. One step one step. If you worry origin this is not productive, not productive. One step one step my dear. People think too much something, create confusion. Solution very simple, be very careful mind does not confuse. Must keep very very simple. Mind likes confuse, give mind job to do.

Rob: *So is it another way of saying that if everybody does the same and disperses it like a tree does, that there isn't really a problem in the first place, that it's just an illusion?*

M: When confusion disperse, become very easy to see problem, then you find solution for that problem. Must disperse confusion first. Like disperse cloud and see sky, this is why do not worry origin - first remove confusion. Many people confuse, there is no solution because they do not know problem. OK?

Rob: *Yes, it is very, very simple.*

M: Yes my dear very simple. You do not need to find solution you just need to find problem but you cannot find problem because there is confusion. You will never find problem when there is confusion because of confusion, so disperse confusion and make more clear. Then very clear. Very clear next step. OK? This applies to everything; this applies to everything, many things.

Mary: *I was just wondering if confusion starts from the same place.*

M: Yes my dear. Always same place, always place of disorder, always wherever disorder – confusion. If disorder in individual life then confusion individual. So all confusion originate disorder.

Because so much confusion, disorder in world so they feel other people, so confusion not individual confusion, not individual disorder, so confusion from disorder, not just only problem in world. Confusion originate same place, does not originate problem world. Problem world disorder but also personal individual disorder also create confusion OK?

27 HOW DO I EXPERIENCE SELF?

Mary: *Right. I am going to go back to the question that I really wanted to ask Master. what has been happening with mind and how people are to understand it? I was reading through how Master said about the beginning of creation and I got a bit confused. I am thinking we need more clarity or different words to describe that because I….*

M: First people need to understand self and then they understand Master. Master explanation very clear, only problem mind not clear. When mind clear, when people understand, one step one step OK? So when mind become more clear - understanding possible. When mind not clear, mind confused, even simple explanation confuse. No problem, no problem. When something appear like challenge, like difficult to understand, then it require little effort to benefit from wisdom. If no effort required people do not even consider to understand explanation because they do not consider important, even they overlook.

Mary: *We come back to the same thing; people have to have a clear mind before they can experience self.*

M: Some people experience self and mind become clear. Some people clear mind and experience self. Different way.

Mary: *When you say experience self are you saying individual self or the origins of where we are created.*

M: Same my dear. When you experience self, question even obsolete because you understand everything. So do not worry.

Mary: *I am still stuck on how I experience self; doing what, being what?*

M: Sometime when you enjoy something very spontaneous, this can feel for you like little bubble, little bubble very excited. So when you feel little bubble try to make explosion. Then this little bubble become complete experience.

Mary: *I understand Master. Thank you.*

M: This is where you find experience self – in bubble. You very familiar with bubble when you become excited, when you recognize bubble, bubble become enormous.

28 CLEAR COMMUNICATION

M: Very important to examine every detail communication. Communication other, communication self. Examine detail, discard unnecessary. Like when you look grain rice and discard mold, sometime rice mold, do not want to eat poison so examine every detail communication self, communication other. Then no poison. No problem. When you examine in detail, mind become more comfortable, more happy. When stomach have mold, stomach have pain. So when mind have mold there is much distress, same stomach. You would not consume rice mold - never, this is stupidity, same mind. Do not consume poison from mind; do not express. For other poison, for self poison also. People very happy to look after stomach. Very important for them to have happy digestion. Whole society value this past-time eating, and forget mind. Forget same process mind.

Mary: May I ask something regarding that Master? In other words we have to be very careful of what we say and how we say it, the quality of our words?

M: Exactly. Words become like arrow. If arrow does not reach target, can injure other. You understand? Target like bulls eye. If arrow does not reach target because focus incorrect, can injure other. This is why precision important, so no injury.

Mary: When you say precision is that to have accurate communication with someone to speak only the truth and what the reason for the communication is?

M: Yes my dear, but bow, you understand bow? Bow from mind not wood - but love. Bow is love.

Mary: I understand. There is very much mis-communication between people, monitoring words; thinking you might hurt the other person. We withhold truth and clarity, saying what we think the other person wants to hear.

M: This is eventually injury, but also same principle applies self. Self thought, self-belief, exactly same. So if belief miss target - injury self.

Mary: The problem is we are not taught how to be kind to ourselves. It is OK to say good things about others but it is not OK to say good things about ourselves.

M: What is problem my dear? Is only habit. When child has good example child copy. When child has other example child also copy. Always habit, so just practice. Requires practice. Requires understanding consequence.

29 HOW DO I HELP MY CHILDREN FIND THEIR DIRECTION?

Annie: *Part of my stress at the moment is that I am battling with my two grown-up children one is eighteen and the other twenty-one; they are just floating around with no direction. What advice can you give me to pass on to them? I just feel that they are not going anywhere and I am so frustrated and I feel like they are going through life and the whole family is walking on glass because we are not sure...*

M: Why do you think family know best? Children know best. Children have own direction. Do not worry children. Do not worry children. They know exactly how they would like to live their life. Is not any concern of yours, is not any concern of family.

Annie: *I feel like a failed mother.*

M: My dear, children love you very much. They would not say you are a failed mother. You must stop worry children. Master already say to you consequence worry. When you worry children, you prevent success. When you love children when you allow children to express self in own way, children become like magnificent creature never seen before. You never even imagine. You do not see inside children. You do not know their potential. Everybody has incredible potential. You try to direct in one direction but you do not care what direction. You want to know direction but you worry when they do not know direction. This is not serving your children one little bit. The only thing to do is something you do quite effortlessly which is to love children. Children have love parent, confidence parent, they find their way and become success and they never lose parent, always love parent. Do not worry, do not create 1000 foot brick wall, because this is what worry can do and is not productive for children, not for self, not for family.

For children society very challenging, very different experience for them, when children contemplate life their conclusion is completely different from yours. You must honor children's individuality. Do not worry, do not worry, because children will not get lost, you worry they will get lost. Do not worry. You tell them you have every confidence they will find their own way. You say these simple things to them. When you say to them "I have confidence you will find your own way", this empowers them to find their own way. Because you give them the direction, this is the direction they need, just to say to them "I have every confidence you will find your own way." This is all they need from you. OK

Annie: *Yes. Thank you.*

Nikki: *I have three children and I worry about them all. I want to try and work out how to relax a bit and let them go their own way.*

M: If you worry children it's like you trap them under dome of despair and gloom so children can see nothing. They do not see whole world, they do not see infinite possibility - because it is like they are hidden under dome, but also very important - rest of world does not see children. So rest of world does not offer opportunities. You must realize this and set them free because when you stop worry – no limitation for children. Children like trees and flower. They grow strong and they grow big but if when they grow and you look down and look at little tree it does not grow because you stand on root. Tree does not get sun because you cast shadow over tree, tree does not get water, because water fall on you, same children, understand? Same children.

Nikki: *Yes, so I need to let them make their own mistakes?*

M: Yes my dear, yes my dear, because everybody become very strong. When tree grow from seed and when find rock in way it grow around rock, does not stop grow, grow around rock, find best way. Same children. You see when tree must bend around rock, tree become very strong, but if you move rock tree does not have to push so hard and lose strength, same children. If you only send love to children, like much sun, then tree grow even bigger.

30 MY HOSTILE NEIGHBOUR

Lynette: *I moved home a year ago and my neighbor is very hostile towards me and I don't understand why.*

M: She is very suspicious of you. This one very suspicious of you. She see you, she form impression of you completely contrary to nature self, she very much mistaken. She view you with such suspicion it make you hesitate to approach this one. All that is required is to show this one she is mistaken. Her suspicion push you away and you even become in other person eye, you behave in such a way to make other person think they are correct. She create this situation with suspicion. You continue situation by reaction. So very simple my dear. You offer friendship in some very small way.

Lynette: *Difficult.*

M: You smile, you offer help when you see you can do so, even you approach this one with a smile on face "what a wonderful sunny day" even something this simple.

Lynette: *It's difficult.*

M: No my dear this not difficult, only in mind difficult. You have ability to fix entire situation. Now you understand problem not complex at all. Only misunderstanding many year, only misunderstanding. This one suspicious because people very unkind to this one.

M: My dear, my dear if you have little animal many times abuse, very difficult for animal to trust someone, so remember this one little damaged by previous experience.

Lynette: *Yes, very damaged.*

M: Yes my dear, but you can fix. Do not appear to this one as though she is correct. Do not allow this one to continue illusion. Because when you befriend this one like no one before, she will be faithful friend to you like damaged animal. Very big gift for you and you give this one gift.

Lynette: *Right. I've got to smile.*

M: You must understand damage.

Lynette: *I did think that, but I thought it would be too difficult.*

M: No my dear very simple. Maybe in time like animal must learn to trust. But be persistent, realize problem, have compassion - do not worry.

Lynette: *I can do it.*

M: Yes, my dear exactly. Exactly.

31 HOW DO WE HELP THE YOUTH?

Directly before the channeling we had been discussing asking Master for a solution to the present unrest and violence prevalent in some of the youth in society. It was channeled that the children are processing unresolved conflict for the world, accumulated from previous generations.

They saw that the world had the problem and not them. They saw that their parents and their grandparents had been quietened down over time and the people had minds like zombies. They were never going to allow themselves to become like zombies and would rather die.

Master said these children are very wise and have answers to help change the world. That the common ground for communication with them was the desire to change the world and we must ask them for their ideas and assure them that we will listen and act upon their ideas. They are frustrated because they have so much passion and no one listens and they have no resources and feel powerless to change the world yet determined not to become zombies.

M: Welcome my dear,

Marie: *Welcome to you too.*

M: You worry, you worry. You worry other people distress.

Marie: *Yes.*

M: Very much worry, worry, worry.

Marie: *Yes*

M: Do not worry. When you do not understand something you have fear, and you worry, but do not worry this problem. These people very much distress, but they do not see distress. They see world crazy. They know all the answers. OK, they see you crazy, they see the world crazy, very angry because no one listen, they know how to fix world, in own head, so they do not feel distress. You think these people big problem, they think you have big problem. OK. They not believe people. They see people like zombies; they have no respect for zombies, so who is crazy?

You think these people distressed, they are not. Their mind is very wise because they understand many problems in world, they do not have resource, they do not have power to change the world. They want the world to change just like you want the world to change. This, my dear, is the common ground.

This is the way forward for communication these people. The only way forward to communicate with people. Understand.

Marie: *How?*

M: This is the only way, the first step. This is the key to the door to understanding between zombie and these, you call them hooligan. Hooligan, hooligan, hooligan. This is what you call them. They not hooligan. They are very frustrated. They try to communicate but how can you communicate zombie – they have no mind. Of course these people angry. Zombie in control of world, they see problem, they do not have resource, zombie have no mind so they do not even listen. They have no capability listen, this is what happen. This is their perspective. No one understand their perspective, but when you understand their perspective, this is intelligence. This is intelligence. They are so finely tuned to the problems in this world, their frustration enormous, They are so capable to effect positive change but no one listen to them. No one listens to them. Of course they angry and frustrated. They see before parent, parent's parent, no one listen. No one listen. Parents become quiet, become zombie, so they see this happen many time before, they resolve never happen to us, never happen to us we will not become zombies, we will die rather than become zombie. This is their passion, and these people have so much to offer. They have so much to offer. Please, please listen these people, communicate, understand their perspective. They want change in the world same like you. This is first step to understand, now you can talk these people.

Rachel: *Should we go around to the schools and talk to them? Should we set up a group for them, a youth center? How do we communicate with them how do we formulate our dialogue with these fantastic ...*

M: You tell them we understand you, we know you want to change world, we want to listen to you. We want your idea. We will act upon your idea. You must become master of own destiny. We do not want you to become zombie. We need your help to change the world. You see at moment people believe they can make decision, they believe they make good decision. At the moment they say 'How can we help these people, these distressed people, these angry people, how can we help them?' This is completely the opposite approach for success.

Rachel: We should be asking the children or the teenagers.

M: Yes my dear, how can you help us change the world, how can you help us talk to zombies, how can you help us wake up. Always, always this is revolutionary thinking for many people.

Rachel: *But how do we gain access to these teenagers when the system, the schools, will think us crazy.*

M: Do not worry my dear. Do not worry my dear. These people have many ways communicate each other. If you approach through establishment, zombie establishment, they do not listen. They need fresh approach.

Rachel: *Like Facebook or YouTube or something like that?*

M: Yes my dear of course my dear. Perfect, perfect perfect. This is perfect because you have free expression, you have instant communication world. Instant communication world. You have no restriction. They understand you immediately. Immediately.

Rachel: *So we can set up a site where, maybe a forum stating that we are there to help them and ...*

M: My dear, my dear, my dear. It is very, very simple. Your little machine tell them everything and then, then you create something because they become very, very interested.

Note: We always record the channelings on a Zoom recorder and Master refers to it as a little machine.

M: OK?

Rachel: *Yes.*

M: They think, "Who suddenly understand us?"

Rachel: *And should we tell them about you Master?*

M: One step, one step my dear. One step, one step, we fix problem together. We do not help these people. They do not need help. Zombie need help.

Rachel: *Yes.*

M: Zombie need help OK?

Rachel: *Thank you.*

M: No problem, no problem. You must create something directly. When something build, you will be approached. You do not need to approach anybody because you will be successful. You will become model for change. People want to learn, to understand what you do.

Rachel: Where do we start if not in an establishment? On Facebook?

M: Yes my dear. Direct communication, only way, only way. No need to conform. When you create something very effective, people approach you. Do not succumb to illusion of ability to create change of position in society - illusion. Understand? You are more than capable. More than capable.

32 PERFECTION v. BEAUTY

Fran: *I am just wondering do you have any practical message to help me more in what I am doing. You said to me last time that I would speak and people would be happy. But I think there must be a bit of growth before I get to that point and I wondered if you had any insight for me.*

M: What is problem?

Fran: *I am not quite sure, but it is as if I have an uncertainty but don't know what that is, maybe it's an uncertainty that I am not ready yet, that I have to achieve something more in me, more than I have done.*

M: Little bit perfectionist?

Fran: *Yes! Just a little. (Laughs)*

M: This is problem, only problem, too much perfectionist. You see, if someone in their house spends all day making sure everything perfect they never leave their house, take such a long time.

Fran: *So just do it. That's great thank you.*

M: This is only problem.

Fran: *Thank you, that's great*

M: And when you stop worry things perfect, you more happy.

Fran: *Yes absolutely .Thank you.*

M: Tree not perfect - tree beautiful yes?

Fran: *Yes, I had not thought that a tree was not perfect.*

M: If you analyze perfection you like symmetry, you like order, you like know outcome even.

Fran: *Yes.*

M: Tree not perfectly symmetrical, tree beautiful, tree bear fruit, you don't know what day but always bear fruit so outcome happen, but you do not know day. So this is problem.

Fran: *That's a great answer thank you so much. It's so perfect.*

M: Yes my dear everything simple, everything very simple. Mind always confuse.

Fran: *Yes, I hear that word a lot in my head.*

M: Mind run, mind run very very fast and get lost and forget, so Master come and remind you and we talk before other people.

Fran: *Yes.*

M: You listen other people and other people confuse. So listen self always listen self.

Fran: *Thank you. It was great.*

33 GENTLE DEATH

Carl: *I've got one more... it's the big question which I was going to ask, what happens when we die?*

M: Be more clear my dear.

Carl: *Well, it seems the human race is really attached to its physical appearance and that's where so many of our problems come from and if people understood death in a different way...*

M: OK, my dear, little confuse. People problems come from mind not appearance. When people mind clear, when people experience heart they have everything they need, they do not fear nothing, they do not fear death they do not fear age - nothing, because they have everything. When you understand and experience the love in heart and your mind is clear suddenly you understand everything. You have no more questions because in one moment you have question - you have answer. Nothing appearance, appearance illusion.

Carl: *I thought I had some understanding of death and I was really shocked the other night because my dad is getting quite* *old and I thought he is going to die and well that'll be it, and then I thought I was tired and when you are tired you don't have a clear mind*

M: People love to die, people love to die if their body not comfortable, they want to go.

Carl: *Yes, I think he wants to go*

M: No problem.

Carl: *The heart can't lose anything can it in the way of connection, whether they are living or dead. It's the same feeling in the heart if the mind isn't getting in the way and causing trouble?*

M: Exactly my dear, exactly my dear. When you do not worry father, much easier for father to die because your love surround him, not worry, so when you worry when father die is difficult for him to find his way.

Carl: *Yes.*

M: So with love is very gentle death, very gentle leave body, very easy, very happy.

Carl: *It must be very difficult for people who are dying to be in a room full of people who don't want them to.*

M: Yes my dear causes much discomfort, for spirit - discomfort for everybody. Many people think, then some people frightened. They do not understand, even though everything changes always, they still frightened. Some people think, they pretend, they think they must do something, must say something and they are not clear with how they feel, so they get confused, very awkward because they do not understand, makes it very difficult for father. When you feel love in your heart and this is all you feel this is same when leave your body, this is all you feel, same feeling same experience, wonderful. No more discomfort, no more mind - just love. So when you have this connection you have this experience on earth you love to die. You love to leave uncomfortable body. Is no difference, life no life. Same, understand? No difference.

Carl: *That's the feeling I get around the way we treat old people in UK and maybe Europe. I think it's difficult, their relationship with their parents, because they don't want them* to die. It seems there are lots of people holding on to old relatives.

M: My dear, children experience love from parent so they don't want parent to die. When they experience love in their hearts they do not need parent, very simple. They understand process and they understand resistance. Do not worry father. Just love.

(The channeling comes to a close and there is general chat amongst us.)

Fran: *Thank you so much, I'm blissed out.*

Carl: *How is it for you afterwards? You look very blissful and free.*

Alison: *I feel good, I mean when he was working on you it was just wonderful and I experienced it as well.*

Carl: *You mean when he was working on me there was a subtext to the conversation?*

Alison: *Oh yes, when he was silent he was clearing you and just connecting you (to love) so you feel different. It's not just the questions it's the experience and the energetic work.*

34 *LOOKING FOR LOVE*

This was an interesting situation. Two cousins had come for guidance and it turned out that although their questions were different there was something that united the readings and the two readings together made a whole. Both girls needed to hear each other's information. The first young woman was mid-thirties and her cousin late twenties in age.

M: Ask, ask, ask, quick, quick, quick.

Kelly: *OK. How can I move forward?*

M: Feet, feet move you forward what do you mean move forward?

Kelly: *How can I get my head straight?*

M: Easy you very unhappy girl, what you want to ask is how can I stop to be unhappy.

Kelly: *Yes that's what I want to ask?*

M: Ok. We have a look. It's like your head stuck in sand. You have expression where your head sticks in sand yes?

Kelly: *Yes.*

M: This is you. Very simple solution - pick head up out of sand and you see clearly what you must do. How do I do that you ask, you have been here a very long time and all you see is dark. Makes us unhappy too because we just want for you to enjoy life. There are many, many things for you to do. One – stop feeling sorry for yourself, waste of time. You could be doing many things in this time, what you have to be sorry about. Nothing! You have your arms, your legs, you have your house, you have everything you need. You have nothing to be sorry about. But you look at other people you think their life better than yours. Not so. Many, many people unhappy too. They pretend. They better pretending than you. They have happy face but inside sad. You sad inside, sad in face and others see and they point and they say "you sad". Why do they do this? They too sad inside but you don't notice that, and then when they point makes you feel worse. This is illusion. Everybody same. Everybody have problem. Everybody have things they must do to make life better. People smiling and sad inside do nothing. They think they can hide their problem. No, their problem come like big volcano one day whoosh, and they get shock, they get big shock. They weren't expecting bad things. They weren't expecting lose their health, lose their job lose their marriage even. Lose everything because they don't look inside, but you my dear you know you sad. You better, you much better place than them because you know you sad, don't pretend like them so now easy for you to do something about it. Do something to make you happy. That's all you have to do - very simple. Now that you can see others same as you, you understand them.

Kelly: *Yes.*

M: You see how easy? Hmm?

Kelly: *Yes.*

M: No problem, you have no problem. You must think: "What will make me happy?" and you must do, and it be very, very easy for you to change. You look at yourself and not at others and suddenly all these people with smiling faces and sad inside look at you and say what has she been doing, what has she done that we have not done, because you change. Others will see you change; it will be like the dark becomes the day. It will be like that in a matter of weeks, you will be a different person. You have no problems my dear. And then you start to smile and then you find what you looking for. Oh yes we know what you looking for, you will find exactly what you are looking for. You will not be on your own don't worry my dear. People want smiling faces that's what they want, that's what you want, that's what others want, very easy be happy. OK?

Kelly: *Yes. Thank you. I know what I think makes me happy and I suspect that's not what really makes me happy. I have lots of fantastic things in my life, but I don't know how to find what makes me smile on the inside. I can't focus. I feel like I'm free falling and nothing to grab on to. I don't know what makes me happy. I don't know how to be happy.*

M: It is like you hide under black blanket and you cannot find happiness because it is hidden under pain. When pain goes happy is there, always there, not look outside for happy, happy inside. Happy hiding, because pain so big doesn't want to hurt no more, so happy hides, afraid of pain, again illusion, illusion. Pain gone, pain past, pain past. Let go. This is how to find happy.

Kelly: *Thank you.*

M: You will find happy. You will find happy. Do not be hurt from past, past is past, will not hurt again. They did not know what they did to you. Hmm?

Kelly: *No.*

M: Not their fault, not to blame, they did not know they did. They had a child but they were too busy to think about what this child would need. They did not know what they did. OK?

Kelly: *OK.*

M: No regret. They not bad people, silly people, not bad people, silly, very silly. OK?

Kelly: *OK.*

M: If parents don't love the children like they should, children must love themselves. Yes? All you need is love in your heart. Does not matter where it come from. OK?

Kelly: *OK.*

M: Just silly parent. Nothing more, nothing more. No problem. Love yourself. Now pain go away. OK?

Kelly: *OK.*

M: And you my dear you be quiet, make a change.

(The girls laugh as Jane is usually far from quiet).

Jane: *I would like to know lots of things in no particular order.*

M: Ask, ask ask, quick, quick, quick.

Jane: *I would like to know why you have chosen to speak now and what your motives for sharing your help are?*

M: OK babies when they are born they do not crawl.

Jane: *Yes, understand.*

M: So time for everything. Time was not right, body was not right, was not receptive not clear, yes? Now we use body. OK other question was motive, motive. Ah! What you think motive? Is to help mankind, you see mankind now very very unhappy. Too many people do things to their brothers and their sisters which are unkind. They can be unkind words unkind deeds, even they kill one another. Does not need to be like this, did not always be like this. We come, there are so many wanting for the world like it was before, but it will never be like it was before, no we hope it will be better, and we come to help you to answer question, to give guidance, just to help because we love you very much. You like children to us and we like parent stand by long time while children make mistake and we wait for children to grow up. But this time children don't grow up, they fight and parent is nowhere to help them so they fight and fight more, more, more so we come now, before too late. Now help is needed, children sometime little bit crazy, do not think they have such good brains, but they do not think. We do not understand sometimes these crazy people but we try to understand. We never live like this never, never, never. So we come to help, OK?

Jane: *Yes. I would also appreciate some understanding and reassurance when I feel or have what others would call insight whether or not it is from another level or if it is from myself and when I should listen and when I shouldn't.*

M: Ok. We understand, we explain. You have many levels as you say. Information comes to you from many places even from yourself even from other level of yourself. When you hear information that does not scare you then this information is truth.

Jane: *OK.*

M: When you have thoughts which make you feel uneasy and afraid, not truth. Easy. OK?

Jane: *OK. Yes, thank you. I would like to know if I am on the right path to obtain my full potential with regard to whatever that may be. And I want to know when I will be getting married?*

M: OK. Two questions. My dear your potential already inside you just need open bag to find what is inside. You go through life holding a bag of gold but you don't know what you hold, but it's there. You know you hold something but you don't know what is inside.

Jane: *How will I know?*

M: Time will realize and when you ready to find out what inside then you will open. Do not worry time not right just yet. Be patient, just a little while longer. You have made great progress in this lifetime. Not little steps - big steps. Already big steps. Much, much to come. We see a little thing needs to be sorted out. You call it your temper. When someone like you has much power a little temper not little. Understand?

Jane: *Yes.*

M: Too much power, little temper, not good. Only when you control this temper, not even control, no, when you understand where anger comes from, then no more temper, then you can look in bag. If you have more power now, not good. Not good for you, not good for world. Huh?

Jane: *Yes.*

M: Power must only be used for good. Only for good, understand?

Jane: *Yes.*

M: Marriage, hmm. Why want marriage?

Jane: [Sighs]

M: Another one, silly parents. Hmm?

Jane: *Yes.*

M: Again same answer. Parents not give you the love, so you must love yourself - the same, the same answer.

Jane: *OK.*

M: Many silly parents. But they like children, they not know what they do.

Jane: *Yes.*

M: Power must only be used for good, only for good understand. Someone must teach the children. The parents can't teach the children, so someone must teach the children. Someone must teach the parents! We must stop the destruction of the world, of the people, of the children. Your world is very special, it is very special, don't forget. More questions?

Jane: *Can you tell me what I can do to stop getting migraines.*

M: Ok. Migraine due to fear. You run like a frightened little rabbit down a dark hole. And you run so fast you do not look behind to see what you are running from. You are so scared, my dear it has gone. Nothing to be frightened of. Past it has gone. You can stop running now. Yes? This is why the pain comes, you want to run so fast and your body does not run so fast. If you are running into a brick wall - you hurt!

Jane: *Yes.* [Laughter]

M: Same. Body does not move. You move to get away from something that you think is chasing you. Nothing is chasing you, nothing to be frightened of any longer. All gone. No migraine. No more, no more pain. OK?

Jane: *Yes.*

M: Very simple, everything very simple solution.

Jane: *So how do I lose 3 stone in weight.*

M: You not happy with your body?

Jane: *No.*

M: Hmm! OK. You want to get thin like stick?

Jane: *Yes.*

M: Hmm. Very strange but we will try and help you.

Jane: *Thank you.*

M: Ok when you run from your body and your body stay still your body try tell you to stay still you don't listen. Body gets big.

Jane: *OK.*

M: This is your answer everything. Sudden fear, running, body stay still. Body can't talk.

Jane: *Yes.*

M: No can't talk, so body gets big. Body says look I'm here do not run away from me. Because body love you. Body want you to stay and look after body but you want to run away.

Jane: *I understand but I do not know what my fear is so how do I confront it?*

M: Does not matter what fear is.

Jane: *Just know that it doesn't exist.*

M: Exactly

Jane: *It makes sense.*

M: We will help you when we see you do same thing again we will help you because we are with you. We know your life difficult at times and you hide behind mask, we know. Not difficult for much longer.

Many surprises coming as soon as you stop running you will see clear challenges. You will love your life, you will not want to run away because you love your life so much. You will have much work to do.

Not much work to be happy. After happy - yes. Simple - be happy. We tell you how. After happy much to do.

Jane: *Good.*

M: Very good.

Kelly: *Hard to do things when you are not happy.*

M: You can do nothing when you not happy. Now because everything you do no good, does not make you happy does not make other people happy. You will help each other.

Jane: *Thank you.*

M: My children, we love you very, very much. You can come again whenever you have a problem we will give you the answer so you do not have to wait.

Kelly: *OK.*

M: You do not have to carry problems anywhere. Because we always give you answer.

Jane: *Would you give advice about or answers to questions that we have that we are not aware that we need the answers to?*

M: What the point, if you not ready to understand something you will not ask question. Only when you ready you get answer. Always been this way, always been this way. How can children learn things they do not understand. They cannot.

Jane: *Yes I understand that.*

M: But you always forget what you need and now very, very quickly all questions get answered very quickly.

Jane: *I have no more questions.*

K: *Well I have a question but I don't know if there is an answer.*

M: Always answers.

Kelly: *I love children and have many in my life I want my own that I have given birth to.*

M: Not too late, not too late, not too late. Your future is created by yourself. You smiling and people will smile and people will find that they like you - only then can you make babies.

Kelly: *This is true.*

M: For baby must come into happy mum. You would not want unhappy baby.

Kelly: *I don't want unhappy me.*

M: You not unhappy much longer, we help you too. We help you too, pain is in the past. Happy part hiding, not hiding much longer.

Kelly: *Very nice to talk to you. I have run out of questions.*

M: My dear you will find in your brain there is a little bit that thinks you did not hear anything that was said to her today and there is a big bit which heard every word and this is the bit of your brain that will do the work. Do not worry, because you will do it. Only little bit thinks she does not know. Little bit is mistaken. Little bit can't think, she doesn't know big bit inside work very hard and will change, yes?

K: *Yes I hope so.*

M: Of course this is how it works. We know this already, we know this already about the brain, of course it works, of course it works.

35 ARE OUR LIVES PRE-DETERMINED?

Rick: *Is everything in our lives pre-determined? So whatever choices we make are they all pre-destined?*

M: My dear, there is particular gift like treasure, for every individual. Imagine you walk, inside earth is treasure - this is like life. Some people find treasure easy, some people go like this. This is choice – this is gift. (Master indicates a wavy road on one side and gift on other side)

Rick: *So do we make that choice?*

M: Yes my dear, and Master make gift.

Rick: *But we do have full knowledge of where we are going when making that choice?*

M: When people make decision, only when they realize outcome decision they see destination.

Rick: *Outcome decision?*

M: Yes my dear. They make decision, then outcome happen, then they observe outcome. Then if they have desire they contemplate original decision, contemplate outcome, then they calculate next step. If they do not contemplate decision, do not prepare next step then they...

Rick: *They go wrong.*

M: They have possibility make mistake, make detour! Not mistake – detour. Never a mistake, because always opportunity for contemplation. Never mistake, always opportunity for contemplation. But always, always always many gift.

Rick: *Many Gifts?*

M: Many gifts waiting.

Annie: *So we only ask Master? Shall we only ask for the gift or do we have to work hard for the gift?*

M: When mind very busy, mind demand, <u>demand</u> decision. Almost like, you have expression gun to head, this is like when mind demand decision. So this is constant battle because gift waiting, gift waiting, but when mind persistent make decision because you do not control mind. Need to focus. So you command mind, you say to mind "Master has many gift hidden, many gift waiting. I command you to help discover gift".

But if gift not hidden then always no discipline mind. If gift not hidden then easy for mind to have gift and have question mind. Then this is dangerous situation because mind is not capable to understand gift. Not capable to utilize gift, not capable to preserve gift. Gift is very special. Must understand importance gift so when mind has no control is very dangerous situation, this is why gift is hidden.

Annie: *That is why we come to this world pure and then we have to go through darkness to be able to understand the light?*

M: Yes my dear, process is like when you have grain rice you remove mold and you keep rice no mold this is same process. In life every situation same process.

Rick: *Why do we lose the connection with the self? We come to this world …..*

M: No this is error. Never connection lost. If connection self lost - then body collapse. What you believe you experience is like when cloud come in front of sun.

Rick: *Yes, you can't see the sun.*

M: Yes but you still feel sun, OK? You still feel sun. Little diminish, but you still feel sun. If you believe self lost makes very difficult to remove cloud because belief no sun, so do not even recognize cloud, so not even try to remove cloud.

Annie: *Just look at sun.*

M: Feel sun! And realize cloud never remain one place, always cloud move, always, always.

Annie: *You give such beautiful explanations for everything. So clear.*

Rick: *And the cloud, what is the cloud? Is the cloud the mind or is there any other thing that comes into our lives?*

M: Yes, only always mind, always mind.

Rick: *Is it the identification with the mind and the body?*

M: This is also mind. When you say identification, then who identifies?

Rick: *The mind.*

M: Mind, exactly.

36 A TEENAGER'S CONCERNS

M: Welcome already we see a problem. You have much talent but it's squashed down inside. This must be removed so your life progress. This makes you very frustrated and angry.

Katy: *YES!*

M: OK. Problem mother, mother squash child. She think she do good job. She think she do what mother should do. But no, she does not know what she do. She does not see what she does. So even mother not near, still inside squash. So Master fix. OK Master fix just one moment.

(Some energetic adjustment is carried out, i.e. using energy to create change in Katy)

M: Now mother gone. You will feel different. Do you feel different now? Do you feel tall, suddenly bigger maybe?

Katy: *YES!*

M: OK, life now begins. Life now begin, no more squash. No more people say "no stop, you can't do that, you can't do that, and you can't do that". Now you can do anything you want. Be very successful, very happy. Now, questions?

Katy: *Will I become successful?*

M: Ah! When tree grow big, then tree has much fruit on tree. OK when tree squash, no fruit. So now you grow like big tree, not worry how this happen, this life process, you cannot stop. Mother stop, mother gone, grow big, grow fruit, very successful. Do not worry how grow big. Because now nothing stop you grow big. Much fruit on tree. Much fruit on tree, nothing stop you my dear. More questions!

Katy: *Love?*

M: My dear your tree grow big, much fruit. You get everything. Everything you get. You get what you want and you get more what you want. Things you don't even think of. You ask love, but you don't know love. Yes?

Katy: *Yes.*

M: You will get love very quickly, very quickly, now you grow big. Little people go, you don't need little people my dear, you don't need little people with little mind. Everything change for you very quickly.

Katy: *Soon?*

M: VERY QUICKLY! Understand?

Katy: *I understand.*

M: Big change, completely life change. Mother very surprise.

Katy: *With what?*

M: Change, very surprise.

Katy: *In a good way?*

M: Oh yes my dear. You don't need mother no more. Do not need for squash. Friend OK, but not for mother squash and mother look daughter and she is surprised. Because she do nothing. You change and she do nothing and she think "How did that happen?" I did not do that. She likes control very much likes control.

Katy: *Yes.*

M: She see you change, surprise, she do nothing, big learning for mother. Everything mother do because she love you very much but she does not realize consequences because her mother same, and her mother more same, all change, all change. When you mother, you not like this, you change now already, no more problem.

Katy: *I don't want children.*

M: Ah! Things change. When tree grow big, tree wants to grow fruit, much fruit, many things, and children. Things you want change as you grow big. Don't worry children, you get everything, you get very, very happy. Little people, go little people - little mind go, do not worry little people.

Katy: *Don't need to worry when they are going?*

M: No. Let it happen. They go. They like ants on feet.

Katy: *I hate ants.*

M: They are like ants on your feet, you don't need little ants on your feet. OK? Much better life. Much better life for you. For you life not yet begin. Today, now life begin. Different life. More questions my dear. Or maybe no more questions

Katy: *I have one more ... my dad; will I ever see him again?*

M: Yes my dear.

Katy: *Does he love me?*

M: Yes, my dear of course. You squash, father love hide. Not gone, hide. When father find daughter he find love again. Ok? If father find love but do not find daughter too much pain in heart because love so big for daughter, no see daughter - love nowhere to go, make pain in heart father. Understand. Father very happy to see daughter. He find love for daughter and his heart happy and your heart happy. Do not worry you can find father.

Katy: *Can I ask another question? When will I get over my old step dad?*

M: He wear very many faces, like mask. OK you see one mask, you see other mask, you see other mask. Very confuse for child. Very confuse. He put bad dream in head. Because mask change all the time. My dear we will take bad dream out of your head. OK

Katy: *Yes please.*

M: This man very confuse, not happy, mind not healthy at all. Mind confuse, mind not healthy. Many masks. So …pain gone, a few tears, no more pain. OK. After a few tears no more tears even, no more dreams. You walk new path, new life. New friends. Everything change, everything happy. OK

Katy: *Yes. Is it going to be difficult?*

M: Explain.

Katy: *Getting to my success, is it going to be difficult?*

M: If you worry you slow down success.

Katy: *OK.*

M: OK, one step, one step, all the time, success. Suddenly you see different things and you say this is what I want. OK. You can go best place for job, for work and you get job. Go to the best place.

Katy: *But I don't even know what I want to do yet?*

M: Aah! you will find, you will find. Like apple fall from tree. Job fall in lap, OK?

Katy: *Yes.*

M: Very simple, do not worry. When apple ready to fall, fall. Job will fall in lap like apple fall from tree. Best place to work, very happy, very success. Friends, good friends.

Katy: *Really?*

M: Yes.

Katy: *I've none at the moment.*

M: All change, all change. Completely change. Inside you completely different now. People look, see different person. Little mind go. Your life very happy. Very happy. Mother learn much, she see you change she learn much. Everything, all mistake from mother before, mother before mother before. Every mistake wipe clean when mother learn from you. When you change mother do nothing, this big lesson mother and mother's mother and mother's mother's mother. Understand? Very important, change very big. My dear you have a little habit.

Katy: *What's that?*

M: We think you need handkerchief, yes.

Katy: *What do you mean?*

M: We see your finger in your nose.

[Katy Laughs]

M: Sometimes, yes?

Katy: *YES!*

M: My dear, this does not befit someone who grow big. Maybe child, maybe child, 2, 3, 4, but not someone who grow big.

Katy: *I'll stop.*

M: Please, when people look they do not want to see finger in your nose. OK. We tell you because we love you, we want everything good for you. Just little problem, little problem.

And when you eat your food, my dear please be gentle be slow you call it... sophisticated.

Katy: *Yeah.*

M: You need look sophisticated for big job, OK? Best job need look sophisticated. So, eating slowly gently, no finger in nose, success OK.

Katy: Yes.

M: You finish, any more questions?

Katy: *Can I ask just one little one? My Nan – is she proud of me?*

M: Your Nan – your mother's mother? She funny woman. She has so much love for you but she think she should not tell you.

Katy: *Why?*

M: She think you get big head.

Katy: *Yes that sounds about right.*

M: But she tell other people, you wonderful, but she does not tell you. Ok. She think you get big head. Mother make mistake, mother's mother make mistake. All finish, all finish. OK

Katy: *Thank you so much.*

M: No problem. We talk many times. You come see Master again. Any time my dear, Master always here to help you OK?

Katy: *OK.*

(Within two weeks Katy was offered a wonderful job opportunity which she accepted and called me to let me know that it really had just "landed in her lap"! and she said "Do you know I really hate ants and I've stopped picking my nose!)

37 *HOW DO I DECIDE?*

M: Welcome my dear. Questions?

Lydia: *I just want to ask about my job.*

M: What about your job?

Lydia: *Am I staying in a good job? I work as a child minder.*

M: Are you happy in this job?

Lydia: *Yes.*

M: Then why ask question?

Lydia: *Do I need to stay in this job if can I get something better?*

M: My dear, when you need an answer to any question it is important to know how to find answer to any question, otherwise you come to Master and ask a thousand questions. Understand? Master teach you how to find answer to every question. Two places from which to make decision – if you make decision in head you never really know if right decision, so you must make decision from heart. You must listen to how your body feel. You think "Ok I have this job, what does it feel like working in this job?" Then you ask the question "What does it feel like to leave this job?" and see how your body feel. So, sometimes the time might not be right to leave job. So you wait until body tell you the answer. Body might feel good this week and next week not too good. So you listen to body. Body give you the answer, give you signals. Different people have different way of listening to their body and for you - you get a little bit excited in the stomach like you call butterflies.

Lydia: *Yes.*

M: Yes, you have had this feeling?

Lydia: *Yes. (laughs)*

M: Exactly, that is special to you – not to anybody else, some people; but for you especially butterflies. So when it's a good decision, you get this feeling and you know you are right. So now you can ask yourself 1000 questions and you will get each time the right answer.

Lydia: *Ok so what if I feel nervous? This is exactly the same feeling.*

M: Nervous is very different feeling. When butterflies are present they cause excitement and happy feeling - very different. When you feel nervous it is very different feeling.

Lydia: *Yes, it's scary.*

M: You know this already. Very different feeling. Scary feeling - then wrong decision or wrong time for such decision. So sometimes wrong time and sometimes wrong decision but always is not the time to act.

38 WHY DO I HAVE PAIN AND TINNITUS?

Marie: *Why am I feeling like this, I have an excruciating pain down my leg, and my tinnitus is really bad?*

M: There is a battle between what you want to do and what you think you ought to do. Whenever there is a battle there is injury. You must tell your army what kind of life you would like and they will do this for you. At the moment half your army are at war with the other half so there is pain and discomfort.

Note: A few days later Marie went for an appointment with a cranio-sacral therapist. Excitedly Marie telephoned me when she returned from her appointment. "Alison you know the channel you are connected to is a very high source, I just wanted to let you know because Robert said exactly the same thing. That my body was having a battle internally. I just wanted to let you know never to doubt your channel because a very highly regarded cranio-sacral therapist said the same thing!" I had no doubt but it helped Marie to get confirmation, what is – is! We are all connected to source in a way that we can interpret the reality of a situation. There is no high or low there is clarity or confusion.

On the following week there was no personal channeling but there was a huge amount of work done on the sadness of the world.

Master's face was in abject pain. "They have had enough of pain." He said that there were lines of people in shackles and they were in pain. The pain has been hidden until now but now it was time to surface and go. Marie had not attended the evening's meditation. In the morning Marie phoned to say she had had a meditation early that morning and had audibly heard chains falling off her ankles and as soon as that happened the pain in her leg disappeared. I then told her about the previous evening's mediation when the people were in pain and in shackles.

39 PROJECTING IDEAS

Mary: *The situation in the home I am living in, a lady also living there seems to think there are elemental spirits that live out there and invade a house and she thinks, there is a belief that there are…..*

M: Yes my dear, but this is of no concern self and this one love fantasy, she love fantasy. When she was child she used pretend even she was fairy. She love this fantasy world, but now she does not enjoy – she become fear. If she desire she can live fantasy world and enjoy, but she create fear. When she was child she enjoy fantasy world and whenever something frighten, she escape into this place, so then she associate fear with fantasy. This is problem. If she realize this happen when child then she can separate and will be able to let go of illusion. Because she feel fear and she escape into fantasy when she child, now to empty she project fear. Before she take fear and escape, now she project fear. Understand?

Mary: *Is that why people out there are creating ascended masters and angelic beings that are going to take care of them. Is that part of the illusion to escape?*

M: This is very similar process. They do not experience self. They have no understanding self and they project self. They disassociate, because for them they cannot believe they have this power, they cannot believe they are capable to be angel - so they create angel.

40 YOUR BODY IS A GIFT

Rob: *Hello Master.*

M: Welcome my dear

Rob: *I want to ask you about my present state of feeling like I am always going into trance, always very tired. Like my consciousness is always going from me, and how I can overcome that and whether it's because I still take medication for depression and anxiety I had a long time ago. What do I have to do to move forward being free and doing whatever I want?*

M: So you feel like you, almost like you fall asleep. Almost like to fall, fall, fall, fall and you want to come back?

Rob: *Yes, switching off I think, sometimes.*

M: And then body become uncomfortable, then body become rigid, is like body is rigid and self wants to expand, self wants to play, self wants to enjoy life. But because body is rigid there is no movement. Body does not move. This is problem. This is self wants to escape body, wants to enjoy, so need to move body so self feel comfortable. This is problem and solution. Need to move body. Need to run, need to dance to spin very fast, move very energetic. Almost like body a little, like ice, when body become move, move, move, move then self does not want to escape. This is only problem. Self is very vibrant, need opportunity to express self, but you do not give opportunity to self to express self. Understand?

Rob: *I have problems with legs so I can't run around. Body is injured, or body seems sort of tired.*

M: OK so legs do not move. Can body do like this? (motions moving quickly side to side from waist)

Rob: *Yes.*

M: Then do this. Must create movement in body. Must create movement in body.

Rob: *Tai chi?*

M: Any movement my dear, because at moment rigid, no movement. Tai chi very gentle very slow. Master prefer quick, because self is very vibrant self needs to express self. You practice and you observe more comfortable and you do not want to escape and is only first step, is beginning, only first step. Must move to allow self to express self. Master always give simple solution. Effective solution, because Master love body Master love everybody. Master happy when self experience love and happy and vibrant.

Rob: *A book I have been reading says that the body is just an illusion and to become obsessed with the body is a waste of time.*

M: You do not have car fall to piece. You must look after body. Body is gift, body is gift. If body is completely beyond repair, absolutely no possibility for body to improve is possible to have experience of self and disregard body. This is where belief body illusion. Is possible, but do not make excuse. Body is not completely beyond repair. Do not make excuse. More happy body, more happy experience self, more exuberant self. Self wants to express self. So with you, you must move. If someone has child and you stand child in one place, say to child do not move; do not speak; do not open mouth. You stay in one place and parent look in book and book says child must stay in one place, child must not talk, understand? Understand? This is not nature of child to stay in one place, is not nature of child not talk. Does not matter book, matter self. Self require happy, require express ecstasy. Self requires to express ecstasy and for you must move.

41 A PROBLEM WITH ALIGNMENT

Cilla's profession was as a stage dancer, but her problem, as she perceived it, was to do with a relationship that had become very distant emotionally and physically because he was working at the other end of the country. However the explanation that followed was so interesting and could apply to many other people' situations.

M: Welcome my dear, Master see little problem, your mind in different direction so when you like in two piece, when you in two piece, then not so ability to contain own power, understand? Ability to contain own power dissipated, power come but you do not utilize power because like vessel broken. OK? So this cause much discomfort, cause, little confusion because you realize this very uncomfortable. You have no real direction because you do not have power, so Master do little adjustment OK? Little adjustment. Very interesting my dear. Master complete adjustment. Master see source problem. When you dancing other people you do something like everybody in line, and one goes this way and one goes this way, understand?

Cilla: *Yes.*

M: When you stand like this many people and then you finish dancing, own body go like this, own body one way one way. So when you finish dancing always, always must make practice become complete self, complete connection power. Must sit like this very straight and feel connection Master. Like this, then you stop like this.

When you dancing formation and you go away, body remember configuration because when you dancing other people you become one entity, you become one entity in consciousness so this can create problem when you go away and remain in this formation. This cause problem self also. You will find when you have this configuration in self only, not other people, in self only, then other people do not see you because you look different, like no relationship with you, understand? Because you not same, you like this so they see you but they do not recognize you, you like stranger to them, so relationship change. So, Master fix. So, you must remember whenever you become one consciousness when you dance other people, every formation affect self, even different formation will have effect of altering identity of self so always after dancing formation other people, always very, very important you must meditate, you must, in front of mirror sit with eyes open, realize you like this - not like this. Very important for life because this can occur repeatedly, so must be practice for self and also when you notice, when you realize other people have same pattern, you can explain other people OK? Because this problem for many, many people who work together as one consciousness. Very good for dancing, not very good for finish dancing. Very good dancing because one consciousness everyone move in synchronicity, move together move perfect, become one. Not good when finish dancing for self. Must realize separation dancing consciousness and self-consciousness so other people see self, do not see unusual, unrecognizable energy. When they see unrecognizable energy there is no connection, they forget you because you do not look same. This is problem for you, so Master adjust. You will find people now see you, they now connect. They do not realize before why they do not understand, they do not even think, or concern themselves with problem - just disconnect very easily because no recognition, this is only problem. So relationship change, even revert and begin new, begin new. So you have question my dear?

Cilla: *I just want to know if this guy Andrew still has feelings for me?*

M: This person when he realize you now self, very happy. Like you know, when you suddenly see someone, when long time no see, you very happy. Like this, he very happy when he see you again like self. So this one relationship like new beginning, like plant - like seed come from earth and grow no obstruction, no obstruction very good earth, very fertile earth no rock in earth so plant grow very straight, very quick, very vibrant, so relationship like this, very new very fertile.

Relationship change. Do not worry relationship because now you give very strong signal of self. Before signal very confuse, signal everybody in group, everybody in group become one consciousness so your signal become very confuse, not own signal. So very confuse self signal, and friend, this man, he like this very much, he like this because it is very vibrant very strong no confusion, he relate this very much, he even when you talk this one you listen this one sound voice, sound very different sound very enthusiastic, very exciting because he respond, he react to your vibrant energy - yourself. You notice this will change very quickly. He respond because he feel and he like, like very strong vibrant self for you. Does not like when separated because you very weak. So this not very compatible for him so this was problem for him, but no more, no more - Master fix.. OK? More question my dear, more question?

Cilla: *How can I be more present in his life?*

M: Now my dear, now you give very strong signal OK this one like strong signal, you do nothing because you like transmitter and he like*(s)* signal. Nothing for you to do. Nothing for you to do. Like, when someone like particular music they listen this music all time OK. This one like strong signal so is very compatible for him. He like very much so you just be self, you just transmit strong signal and this one respond. Nothing for you to do. Only remember practice. Only remember practice when finish dancing, when separation has occurred with other people because one consciousness, so when finish practice, always remember to revert to become self, to connect self. This only thing you need to you. You see when you are a magnet you do nothing, understand? Magnet does not need to tell nail I am here I am a magnet. Nail feel magnet and then jump magnet. Magnet do nothing because this is quality of magnet. Now quality of self, very powerful, very strong, transmit very vibrant energy and other one like very much. So you become like magnet, you do not need do nothing OK. More question my dear?

Cilla: *No I don't think so. Just wanted to know if he will come to me if he ......*

M: My dear, my dear we explain, when you talk, you listen change, and you realize this one like very much OK?

Cilla: *No more questions.*

M: You very happy now because now you realize how to control own energy. You learn to control own energy you remain very vibrant even dancing better because when one formation affect energy you go do other formation then very difficult to make transition, because already like this but when you do practice and you become self when you experience own power very straight, when you have to do different formation then transition very easy. Understand? So everything fix, relationship fix, dancing fix, self fix. Self very confident because you realize you very strong magnet do not have to do nothing. Realize own power. Realize own power and teach other people. You can teach other people because you understand this important information for other people, OK? OK my dear.

Cilla: *Yes.*

42 THE GIANT WITHIN

M: Welcome my son. Master see problem. You have big body but inside you hide.

Drew: *Yes.*

M: Master see you hide; you try to make yourself so small nobody see you. You want to achieve much in this world but how can you achieve when you hide? And you very good hiding. You very good hiding, you make yourself very small. Now Master can help you if you agree. If you would like Master make little adjustment

Drew: *Yes please. I would appreciate that.*

M: But my dear you must realize no more hiding OK?

Drew: *OK*

M: You like genie, you hide so much and when Master help you then you like giant. You come out and everybody see you and whole life change. People will look at you and wonder "Who is this man? We never see him before." Hmm my dear very different.

Drew: *Can I ask, Master?*

M: Yes my dear.

Drew: *What is it that you are seeing that is different?*

M: Giant. Master see you big, everything look very different

Drew: *OK. Thank you.*

M: You are big now, you adjust self little bigger, little bigger, little bigger, come back, come back, come back. At moment little adjustment as giant get used to expansion. Now giant very capable control own size, so is at moment little play, little bigger, little smaller, just momentary play. Understand?

Drew: *I understand.*

M: Not exactly stable. Has discovered suddenly not confined so is changing, little changing. This will be moments, only moments. No more hiding.

Drew: *No Master, I don't want to hide anymore.*

M: No not possible, because you cannot get giant into such small space.

Drew: *Do you think I will be able to handle the new responsibility that comes with this? Am I capable?*

M: My dear, more than capable. You will enjoy so much; will not feel like responsibility, will not feel like effort - only joy, only happy. Because has been long time, very long for him. So much joy, much joy.

Drew: *Master can I ask, this hiding, have I been like this in just this lifetime or previous lifetimes.*

M: My dear, my dear, my dear. What importance this question? No importance, no importance, no importance at all.

Drew: *So just to focus and live in the present.*

M: No. No even focus, no effort required. No effort required. Giant so happy. This is essence of giant. No effort.

Drew: *Master can I ask you please?*

M: Yes my dear you can ask many questions.

Drew: *Master may I ask who do you serve?*

M: My dear, my dear son, Master help everybody, this is Master job. Master help everybody because Master love everybody. Only love, and help everybody. Only purpose Master.

Drew: *And is Master part of my consciousness and all other consciousness.*

M: Master is consciousness everyone, and everyone little bit Master.

Drew: *OK, thank you. I'd like to ask Master if you feel I have fully tapped into my healing ability.*

M: No, no my dear. This one only just begin. You do many things. You listen many people. You never experience self you never experience giant. So all knowledge you learn other people very little compared to own knowledge. Now you begin knowledge, become unlimited my dear. Unlimited! You do not need teacher no more because this giant has ability to grow very big indeed. This giant can expand across whole universes and gather information, whenever information is required; this giant has capability to find information directly. So my dear journey only just begin.

Drew: *Thank you I understand. I was going to ask you what can I do to awaken my potential but I think you've already touched on that.*

M: Already awaken!

Drew: *Yes. So the next thing I'd like to ask you is how can I best serve my family – my immediate family?*

M: Already done, my dear already done. Now you very different. You not hiding, you giant. You have capability to get all information you require, you have capability to get more than information you require, so because you change from being small and hiding, this has very dramatic effect on your family, also no effort required. Because very big effect on family. You see, they see you but they do not see you, before, they do not understand, you are like doctor, you carry bag of doctor. You ready to help them but they have no value because you hiding. You no longer hiding my dear. Family have much respect for you. They have much respect for you and they will clamor, not just ask but clamor to ask for help. Understand?

Drew: *Yes I understand.*

M: Very different. Very different situation.

Drew: *Yes.*

M: You have knowledge, you have understanding. You have capability of finding more information and this they will see. You will be revered, my son, revered. Understand? Very different. Not family you know. Not family you know. Very different. So they will ask. It will be very clear, method that you choose to help. You time will be very precious to you because of the demand. OK?

Drew: *Yes.*

M: So you must be very careful. You must be discerning and you must, in your mind you must decide important request, not important request, because demand so big, you cannot be running here, there, everywhere. Very important, be discerning importance of requests, because, you my son you want to help everybody. This is your nature to help everybody, but when demand is great you must be very discerning and help those with greatest need. OK?

Drew: *Yes. I'd like to ask regarding family in the sense that none of us siblings, as we are getting older, none of us have children. I am just wondering for myself whether I am doing* *something subconsciously not being in a relationship and creating a family of my own. What do you think?*

M: *My dear, when you hiding no one see you. So now relationship, family very possible. Before not possible, all that change, very possible my dear.*

Drew: *Now that's really clear. Thank you. I'd like to also ask, I've been working in the same job for many years in one building and I always thought I was there for a reason but I no longer feel this and I am wondering what is it that is keeping me there?*

M: *My dear do you not see, your work is exactly the same problem. Where you work you were not seen. Others were seen, not you. Understand?*

Drew: *No, I don't sorry.*

M: *Inside you hide, in work when people come, who they come to see. Do they come to see you?*

Drew: *Not directly.*

M: No my dear, no so this is exact reflection of inside. Understand?

Drew: *I understand.*

M: Job not required anymore. Now you understand, now you not hiding, things change very quickly my dear, much demand for you.

Drew: *Wow, yeah that was really clear. I can understand now being in environments on a daily basis surrounded by 1500 people, it's like a needle in a haystack, I guess being in that environment and hiding.*

M: Hmm.

Drew: *Yes hiding amongst all those people.*

M: But even they do not come see you.

Drew: *No. No they don't. No they don't.*

M: Very important now they come see you. They come see giant.

Drew: *It is, yes I can understand that. I used to dance as a profession and I felt that was an amazing way for me to express my inner self, my creativity. I don't dance anymore professionally and not really for fun, but can I ask you if you think that is something I should still be doing in some way?*

M: My dear, when you dance before, the experience of joy from dancing is because you begin to feel like giant. Your energy, you fill a bigger space around you, understand, and you begin to feel like a giant and then when you finish dancing you hide again.

Drew: *Yes that's right.*

M: That's why you enjoy this experience much, because you needed to become giant, so you experience little, little bit, you dance, you feel big, you feel wonderful, but you do not understand this is what you need all the time and you hide. Now no more hiding. You giant. So dancing not important not important for experience. If you enjoy dancing then dance.

Drew: *OK. It doesn't necessarily fill a bigger potential for me now.*

M: Only reason you feel so good dancing is to experience giant.

Drew: *That makes sense. OK thank you Master. Another question I have is I feel as though I am a quite receptive person regarding energies around me. I practice, or am interested in a few spiritual teachers and I am not holding onto any direct spiritual practice but take much from many practices and I feel in myself, divided and don't know which path I should follow.*

M: OK my dear, Master already explain little. You need follow no path. You spend much time, you learn things you get knowledge. Now you have ability know everything self. You do not need teacher. Giant can grow big and when giant grow big, giant encompass all knowledge.

Drew: *OK.*

M: Like fisherman throw net into water and gather in fish. When giant grow big, gather much knowledge. For you this very easy. You do not need teacher you do not need path. These things confuse. OK no one follow, no path. Experience giant, experience self only, because my dear is all you need.

Drew: *Will this experience be clear for me? Sometimes I experience things and they are not too clear. Will it be totally clear for me?*

M: Yes my dear, you not hiding no more. Now giant has come, giant go back no more, it cannot become tiny and hide again. Impossible. You cannot bring lion and say to lion: "there is a little mouse hole, go into mouse hole lion. No my dear not possible, not possible".

Drew: *Thank you. I think my final question would be I am concerned regarding this spate of knife stabbings on young people at this moment and I wondered if it was a karmic thing for those individuals and if there is something we can do to change this or to stop this?*

M: For this unfortunate situation is not one solution for all. Each individual their pain come from different place, so different solution required, many very confused, many very lost, they do not know. They need much love, they need so much love my dear, so much love. This is big problem because things are changing very quickly. Some people do not understand, they do not look for answers, they do not understand this way. They realize many problems but they never look self, always look other people, they blame other people always. So they think if they remove other people, problem go away. No! Always answer self, but these people do not understand, so even people little they try to help situation even these people not clear, even these people confused. Little, little, like self, understand? People like self, love people, you help. Only people like self have ability to help this situation because other people do not understand, they do not understand process self-examination, they do not even understand love other people, even this they do not understand. They like angry man, angry, angry man they do not care about nothing, they have no love. In time my dear these people will receive love. Little time when Master has big army like yourself. OK Understand. Master send big army of love to help everyone ... This is solution, only solution.

Drew: *Thank you Master. I am finished questions and thank you thank you thank you for sharing knowledge.*

M: My dear you are very wise, very special wise giant, much work to do, people have much respect for you, they never tell you because they never see you. Very different now. Very different now. Nothing to worry. Your heart sing. And whole life sing. Do you understand how important when giant sing?

Drew: *Yes.*

M: Yes my dear, yes my dear

Drew: *Thank you.*

43 ABOUT CREATING OUR REALITY

Mary: *So Master is it a fact that everything we perceive, the people that come into our lives, the situations that are created around us - we have to take complete responsibility and not worry about other people and what they are doing. It's me doing that to me?*

M: Do not worry explanation. Life happen. Life happen like flower open, like tree grow, life happen. If you try to analyze to extreme is not productive for you; is not necessary for you to analyze but enjoy. When you analyze to extreme is like you see little seed grow, you remove one grain earth, you remove other grain earth, eventually no earth and seed die, cannot grow because you undermine surrounding.

Mary: *I understand.*

M: Less analyze, more stability, more love and seed become magnificent. Do not need to move earth.

Mary: *I guess I need to understand more the process of life. I have the understanding that we make life happen.*

M: This is misconception. To have desire is enough. To force situation, is destructive. When you have desire to enjoy life this is like when you see beauty in flower and body become overwhelmed. When this desire flow every aspect life, then you create garden full of flower. When you try to design garden - not so beauty. Understand?

Mary: *Yes.*

M: At moment people believe they create reality but, if you have someone who has responsibility to design structure, tower, bridge, something, this is their responsibility but they never study design, not even for one day, but they believe they create reality so they forge ahead to create imperfect structure. So when foundation is knowledge, wisdom, love you can create beauty.

Mary: Right. I understand that when it comes to perceiving ourselves as we truly are, the internal self, but in the world that has been created around us there are what we call practical issues, people have to go out and earn a living and specialize in certain fields in order to bring in the money in order to be able to survive in this system that has been created. And I think that is where misunderstanding happens; where people feel they have to be in complete charge of their lives in that direction.

M: *Yes my dear, Master understand concern. But, if you build tower with brick like child and tower is not perfect, it begin to lean. Even if you try to correct lean, eventually tower topple. Always foundation must be correct in order for stability. Always. Only way to correct is to begin new.*

Mary: *OK.*

M: Must focus foundation. Perfect foundation always consist wisdom love.

Mary: *I understand, thank you. Can we ask more questions? Especially based on what we have been discussing Master I have a question from Alison from what we have been discussing earlier on. Alison would really love to do what Master has decreed for her to do, that is to speak to the rest of the people. Not quite clear how that is going to fit in with what practical problems that are confronting Alison at the moment.*

M: Problem this one has much love, much knowledge, much wisdom but she does not build tower. Is very capable to build tower. There is foundation, stability, but she is so fear to build tower topple, she does not build tower. Always she see tower topple so there is fear to re-create. Is possible even to remain inactive, but people need example. Tower does not topple. Needs courage. This one must design tower, must take action to construct tower. Is more than capable. She wait for instruction but forget she must give instruction, must become General. She desire greater authority, what use when no action. Must take action, must take action. Simple. Very simple solution. When this one build tower it become tall, never topple, people look tower and they want to know how to build same.

44 ABOUT MASTER'S PLAN

Rick: *Master you said not everyone was ready for self-realization. Is there any group of people that are going to be excluded from ......?*

M: No my dear, no my dear, if you prepare feast you have family at table you do not feed everybody except this one. OK? Everybody in family share feast. If you exclude there is no solution, no transformation.   Is not possible for transformation with exclusion. Is not possible. Is not love. Is not love. Remember -

"Bea-u-ti-ful in-stan-tan-eous phe-nom-en-a!"

ABOUT THE AUTHOR

A brief account of the sequence of the events in my life which led up to that moment in March 2008.

I was aged around twenty when I heard about Stonehenge and ley lines. As I recall it, this is the first time I thought about energy travelling in lines and decided that I would try, with my conscious thought, to make a ley line in my house. So I stood in my living room sending my thoughts in a line across the room and back again and figured that if I could do this well enough then someone would come and trip over the line! It didn't work! This was my first and last attempt at creating a ley line, but looking back at this time of my life it was a time when something woke within me, an interest in "something else" beyond the ordinary daily life of going to work and bringing up a family.

By then my first born son was one year old and at nursery. While I worked in an office, his father attended Westminster University studying Physics and I too became interested in the subject. We had wonderful conversations and I realized that anything was possible, that we create limits in reality only when we create limits in our thoughts. I have always, as far back as I can remember, remained open minded and all my learning has come from experience, recognising that if you build walls around yourself they block your view. At the same time I remained as intellectually sceptical as the next person.

Elusive Love

Around the age of twenty-five a friend of mine who suffered with migraine headaches pleaded with me for help. Not having a clue how I could help, I asked him what on earth he wanted me to do! He asked me to squeeze his head; he wanted me to do anything to take the pain away. I stood behind him as he sat in a chair, placed my hands on his head and to be honest I closed my eyes through boredom, but what I saw was bright light. He asked me what I was doing because the pain eased, then it returned and then it eased again. We figured out that when my eyes were closed and I was looking at the inner light, his pain subsided. So I just stood there, eyes closed in this manner until his pain had gone.

Over the following years when any one of my friends had a headache I would say "Oh, I can get rid of that" and proceeded to hold their head in the same way. It worked every time and for me it was a game. I had never heard of healing, I was young and just didn't really pay it any attention.

Then in 1985, some nine years later and at work one day, Debbie my boss noticed that I wasn't doing what I was supposed to be doing and was standing in the kitchen with a colleague, my hands placed upon her head, my eyes closed. Out of respect she did not interrupt. I was very aware of her tiptoeing around me and at the same time concerned that I might get the sack, but I carried on until I felt an easing in my colleague's head! When I had finished, Debbie asked me what I had been doing and I told her that I had been getting rid of my colleague's headache.

Debbie explained to me that I was a natural healer. She told me too that she was a member of a group which met once a week to meditate for personal development and distant healing at The Lilleth Healing Sanctuary & Spiritualist Church in Ealing, West London. She invited me to come along one day as a guest. I was intrigued and took up her invitation. After a few weeks of attending as a guest, the group invited me to join as a regular weekly member. For the first few years this was the only time when I could relax, feel safe, accepted and heard. I felt I could cope with the week ahead and my regular contact with the group gradually enabled me to find my inner strength within the peace and stillness of our meditation sessions. The inner light I saw within me when healing people was present when meditating and over time it grew in intensity.

Until recently I had never attached any significance to outward appearances or ritual, so the customs of the people who attended the church and the entire set up of services etc. were of little importance because I was gaining so much personally. That was the only consideration I had when I reflected upon my association with the group.

My passion and sole purpose became to work with the healing gift I knew was there. Sometimes I had five part-time jobs to allow the flexibility of time to fit in my clients and it was the healing that took over as my main life interest …. healing myself, my family and others. Whilst at the Lilleth, I began to develop clairvoyantly, that is I was able to "see" with the third (or inner) eye; images would appear in my head much like dream images but I would be wide awake. During a healing session I developed an ability to "see" images which seemed to originate within the subconscious mind of the client and also see what seemed to be the energy within and surrounding their body. The images were always relevant to their past or present situation or health problem.

During a healing session I would observe and encourage the images to change from a negative to a positive scene or from black to white or, if colours, expanding or getting more vibrant. I tended to specialise in emotional and psychological issues as my ability to "see" representations of the content of the client's subconscious mind made it easy for me to use the light energy to change the images viewed. In turn, the healing seemed to change the client's state of mind to the positive which created subtle yet tangible transformations in their lives. It seems as though, much like updating a computer and running an anti-virus programme that their inner programming gets cleaned and upgraded to a much better version, one that runs more efficiently and happily.

I began to intuitively know things relating to the health of the clients. Information flooded to me during every healing session corresponding to each individual in specific ways while simultaneously receiving information pertaining to homeopathic remedies, diet and allergies, mineral deficiencies, aromatherapy combinations and crystals among a variety of other very specific information. Since about 1990 I have been intuiting precise homeopathic remedies for clients and then about ten years later while working on a client, I observed the misty figure of a gentleman standing next to my treatment couch; he was dressed in a suit from the 1800's, his hair was smoothed down and parted in the middle. He introduced himself to me saying: "Dr Johnson. We have been working together for some time now but have never been formally introduced". He was a homeopath and was the one who had been advising me on remedies for my clients.

I decided to put Dr Johnson to the test. A homeopath associate I knew examined me one day and within thirty minutes of being given a 'first name' only, I correctly identified the remedies for eight out of ten of her clients and the other two remedies I suggested proved more suitable than the ones she had chosen. She remarked that she had not yet studied those two particular remedies.

During one period of my life in about 1998 I was woken in the early hours of the morning with a compulsion to write poetry. The words flowed into my mind so rapidly that I would have to use my computer to type as fast as I could, often writing for many hours. This only happened during the night, but produced over a matter of only three weeks, hundreds of poems many of which were in a pre-1900 dialect. I began to think and speak in rhyme and carried on writing over the years although not so prolifically.

The following years encompass many other exciting developments on my spiritual journey. I took several classes in various healing modalities, each of which helped more and more to clear my own personal issues, improve my overall health and make me a clearer channel for healing others. I also studied Shamanic practices with Siberian shamans and developed a keen interest in Sacred Geometry. I visited various spiritual teachers to receive their blessings (darshan) such as Mother Meera, Karunamayi, and Amma .

Along with a handful of friends I started a meditation circle in January 2008. There were some participants who had many years of experience of meditation and others who were relative beginners. Over the first few months people came and went until the energies within the group stabilised and began to gel. The experiences we all had and the rapid progress we were making was extraordinary.

In March of 2008 during a visit to Mother Meera whilst she was in Roehampton, UK, I received 'darshan'. Darshan is the experience of being in the presence of a guru or self-realized person. On walking back to my seat I thought "Oh well that wasn't much, needn't have come really". Over the next few minutes as I quietly sat in meditation, eyes closed, I inwardly saw myself as a column of light enclosed in four metal bands. The bands were removed and my light body expanded rapidly and then shot up like a rocket. I felt fantastic, free and expanded.

The following week in our meditation circle my body was taken over by a powerful presence. The presence spoke using my voice box but with a very deep voice. I remained aware of the presence, rather like I was waiting in the background. My arms and legs shook rapidly and uncontrollably. It was quite strange, and I did not know what was happening, but allowed it to continue because I felt completely safe. The consciousness explained that it was 'Zadkiel', a name I had never heard before. My great friend Marie had read about Archangel Zadkiel and said she definitely felt there was an angelic presence in the room. Zadkiel came only the once as if to "open the gates" to a higher consciousness. The following week during our meditation, again my arms and legs began to shake, my foot rapidly tapping on the floor and my arms quivering. I was told that the entity/consciousness was anchoring into my system and my body shook because it was adjusting to receive the incoming energies. Over the following few weeks as I entered into the trance state the shaking gradually subsided and each week my body felt more comfortable as the transition into the trance state became more fluid and less dramatic.

At our next meditation session, a new consciousness entered my body and communicated that it was the Consciousness of the Collective Soul. "He" spoke with a Chinese accent and explained that "he" had been the teacher of Lao Tzu and Confucius. "He" said Lao Tzu understood everything and Confucius had asked many questions. "He" referred to himself as Master and explained that "he" had never incarnated on Earth. It is my choice to refer to the voice as "he" for ease of explanation. My understanding, as it was later explained to me, is that this energy is a part of the consciousness of us all as a collective, not of a separate being.

Yet again the next week while sleeping at night, I was awoken in the early hours of the morning. This time it was not poetry flooding into my head but the voice of Master. He told me to record everything he said, as his information was for everyone. Over the next few pages you will find text that is word for word what was channelled to me that night. Thereafter I recorded everything as far as possible, except for one or two evenings when the recorder was switched off by mistake. When that happened I typed up the received information to the best of my ability as soon as I got home from the meditation circle.

Throughout my spiritual development I have never sought anything but the peace and serenity that meditation brings. I believe it is that openness and acceptance of all that I have experienced rather than taking on beliefs that are taught by others that has enabled me to be the clear channel that I am for the energy and information that I am blessed to receive and transmit to be used to help others.

During the years after Master first became known to me I have had the most extra ordinary experiences and revelations in my meditations and with clients in their healing sessions

I presently see people individually and in groups to enable their personal questions to be answered and those answers are always given in an atmosphere of total love, compassion and complete understanding. When people come to see me I always suggest they arrive prepared with questions but invariably Master speaks first. He already knows their problems and speaks directly about their issues before anyone has time to ask questions. Often visitors never finish asking the questions they bring along because with a few simple words Master can erase their anxieties and open their hearts to experience the energy of pure love.

If you wish to be kept informed of public events and future book publications please email

alison@voicesofthesoul.com

www.voicesofthesoul.com

Made in the USA
Charleston, SC
12 February 2016